William Henry Giles Kingston

Adventures in Australia

William Henry Giles Kingston

Adventures in Australia

ISBN/EAN: 9783337177904

Printed in Europe, USA, Canada, Australia, Japan

Cover: Foto ©Andreas Hilbeck / pixelio.de

More available books at **www.hansebooks.com**

ADVENTURES IN AUSTRALIA

ADVENTURES IN AUSTRALIA

BY

WILLIAM H. G. KINGSTON

AUTHOR OF "GREAT AFRICAN TRAVELLERS," "SHIPWRECKS AND DISASTERS AT SEA," "DIGBY HEATHCOTE," &C.

WITH THIRTY-FOUR ILLUSTRATIONS

LONDON
GEORGE ROUTLEDGE AND SONS
BROADWAY, LUDGATE HILL
NEW YORK: 9 LAFAYETTE PLACE
1885

Mr. W. H. G. KINGSTON'S
TALES OF ADVENTURE IN ALL QUARTERS OF THE GLOBE.

ADVENTURES IN THE FAR WEST. With coloured Frontispiece and 36 Illustrations.

ARCTIC ADVENTURES. With coloured Frontispiece and 40 Illustrations.

ADVENTURES IN AFRICA. With coloured Frontispiece and 42 Illustrations.

ADVENTURES IN INDIA. With coloured Frontispiece and 36 Illustrations.

ADVENTURES IN AUSTRALIA. With coloured Frontispiece and 34 Illustrations.

KIDNAPPING IN THE PACIFIC; OR, THE ADVENTURES OF BOAS RINGDON. With coloured Frontispiece and 23 Illustrations.

LIST OF ILLUSTRATIONS.

	PAGE
NATIVE BEE-HUNTERS	5
"SOME RASCALLY BUSHRANGERS 'STUCK ME UP'"	13
A NATIVE DANCE	17
THE ROCK KANGAROO	25
A NATIVE VILLAGE	29
THE KANGAROO	37
"FEEDING THE INHABITANTS OF MY FARM-YARD"	41
OPOSSUM HUNTING	49
"SEATED BEFORE A SMALL FIRE, ENGAGED IN COOKING"	57
"EACH HOLDING IN HIS HAND A THROWING-STICK"	63
"THEY WERE TWO WHITE LADS WITH A COUPLE OF DOGS"	69
"CRACKING OUR WHIPS AND SHOUTING"	75
"I CAUGHT SIGHT OF TWO HORSEMEN"	81
"THREE KANGAROOS LEISURELY CROPPING THE GRASS"	89
STUCK UP BY BUSHRANGERS	95
"HE MIGHT HAVE BEEN MISTAKEN FOR A BRONZE STATUE"	101
"BRAVE CARLO SPRANG UPON HIM"	113
"GUY BENDING OVER THE PROSTRATE FORM OF A MAN"	121
"ROUND AND ROUND THE TREE THEY CLIMBED"	129
"KNOCKING DOWN WITH THEIR BOOMERANGS SOME LARGE BIRDS"	137

LIST OF ILLUSTRATIONS.

	PAGE
"SOON HAD SEVERAL SECURED BY THEIR NECKS"	149
"TOBY STANDING WITH HIS KNIFE IN HAND"	163
"A SAD END OF A MIS-SPENT LIFE"	169
"OLIVER AND RALPH SENT A COUPLE OF SHAFTS INTO ITS BODY"	173
"WE CAUGHT SIGHT OF THE HEAD OF A PERSON RISING ABOVE THE GROUND"	177
WOMBATS	181

ADVENTURES IN AUSTRALIA.

CHAPTER I.

SOME years ago two travellers, mounted on wiry yet strong looking steeds, were wending their way through a forest in Australia. They were both young and dressed much alike in broad-brimmed pith hats, loose red shirts, corduroy trousers and high boots with spurs.

Each of them had stuck in his belt an axe, a brace of pistols, and a long knife; while at his back was slung a serviceable-looking rifle, showing that they were prepared to defend themselves, should they encounter any treacherous blacks, a very possible contingency at that period of the country's history.

They were followed by an active native also mounted, who led a horse carrying their baggage. The scenery was not especially attractive, indeed so great was its sameness that alone they would have been utterly unable to find their way. On either side rose tall stringy-bark and other gum trees, their curious and narrow leaves affording scarcely any shelter from the rays of the almost vertical sun, the huge white stems from which the bark hung down in ragged masses giving them a weird and dreary aspect. Tracks there were, but they branched now in one direction now in the other, and were more calculated to bewilder the travellers than to guide them aright. Their map—for being new arrivals in the country they carried one—told them that they should soon reach a broad stream. They were now looking out eagerly for it, wondering whether they should have to wade through it or should find a ferry-boat ready to take them and their animals across.

I may as well say—having thus begun, after the fashion of a writer whose pure and wholesome works I used heartily to enjoy in my boyhood days—that one of the travellers was myself, Maurice Thurston, and the other my brother Guy, a year only my senior. We had lately lost our father, with whose sanction we had settled some time before to come out to Australia and seek our fortunes. We, our mother, our two sisters, and another brother, had been left with a very limited income; and Guy and I, wishing to push our own fortunes and establish a home for the rest of the family, agreed that no time should be lost in carrying our plan into execution. As soon therefore as our mother's affairs had been settled, we set sail from England, and, about two weeks before the day I am describing, arrived in Australia. We had not come entirely on a wild-goose chase. A cousin of our father's, Mr. Oliver Strong, had long been settled in the country, and had replied to an application made to him some time before by our father, saying that he should be happy to receive us and put us in the way of doing well for ourselves, if we were sober, steady, strong, active, willing fellows with heads on our shoulders and without any " fine gentleman " notions.

We were now making our way towards his station, some hundred miles in the interior. Though we had not ridden far from our camping place, the intense heat of the sun made us feel very thirsty, and sympathise with our horses which must have been equally so; thus we were anxious as soon as possible to reach the river, where we hoped to find an abundance of water.

From our black guide we could not obtain much information; for, although we were well assured that he spoke English when we engaged him, we found that it was of a character which would take us some time to learn. However he understood us better than we did him, though we had to put questions in all sorts of ways and repeat them over and over again. We then had to puzzle out his replies, not always arriving at a satisfactory conclusion.

Guy frequently stood up in his stirrups and looked ahead, hoping to catch the sheen of water. At last we began to have some uncomfortable suspicions that, although our black attendant professed to know the way, he had managed to lose it—a circumstance not at all unlikely to occur—and that we were wandering far out of our proper course. Though the sun was of some assistance, yet we might be going too much to the north or too much to the west, and might pass a long way off from the station which we wished to reach. All we could do therefore was to exert our wits, and, should we have got out of the direct path, to try and find it. At length the foliage before us became somewhat thicker, but no sign of water did we see. We were riding on when a loud cry reached our ears.

"There's some one in distress!" I exclaimed.

"I fear that you are right, we must find out," answered Guy.

We were urging on our horses, when a peal of mocking laughter seemed to come from the wood close to us.

"What can that be?" I asked; "some natives who want to frighten us, or an unfortunate maniac."

The shout of laughter was repeated.

"Him one jackass!" observed our guide, Toby.

"Jackass! What can the fellow mean?" cried Guy.

Then looking up we discovered a large bird not far off who was evidently uttering the extraordinary sound we heard. It was, as Toby told us, a laughing jackass, or a gigantic kingfisher. So ridiculous were the sounds that we could not help laughing too.

Presently a number of cockatoos, rising with loud screams just before us, flew over the trees to pitch again not far off. As we were watching them we found ourselves at the top of a bank, some thirty or forty feet in height. Below it, to the right and left, stretched a sandy bottom scarcely less than half a mile in breadth, and on the opposite side rose another bank. Below the one on which we stood was a stream of water, flowing sluggishly along, scarcely twelve feet wide, and so shallow that we could see the bottom.

NATIVE BEE HUNTERS.

"Can this be the river we were to come to?" I exclaimed, examining the map.

"No doubt about it," answered my brother; "perhaps sometimes this broad bed of sand is covered, and if we had found it so, we should have had considerable difficulty in crossing; so it is as well as it is, here is water enough for ourselves and our weary beasts." We accordingly agreed to stop and dine. Having watered our horses, we hobbled them and turned them at liberty under some trees where grass was growing; then unslinging our guns, we went in search of the cockatoos we had seen. I killed one, and Guy a parrot; but the report of our guns frightened away the birds, which were more wary than usual, and we had to return satisfied with this scanty supply of food. On reaching the spot we had selected for our camp, close to the water where our black boy was waiting for us, we found that he had during our absence made a fire, at which we cooked the birds, Toby devouring the larger portion.

We would gladly have eaten some fruit, however sour it might have been, but none was to be found. We had just finished masticating the tough parrot, when we caught sight of two natives scampering along as if they were mad, so it seemed to us, for they had their eyes fixed in the air and appeared regardless of all impediments in their way. We shouted to them, but not hearing us, on they went, now leaping over the fallen trunk of a tree, now rushing through a bush, now tumbling into a hole, still keeping their eyes fixed on the object which engaged their attention. We asked Toby what they were about.

"Dey huntee bee. Soon catchee!" he answered. The reply was intelligible enough, but why they should hunt a bee puzzled us. They however stopped, while yet in sight, under a large tree, the stem of which they began to climb. Hoping, as was really the case, that they were going to rob the hive of its honey, we followed them. As we approached we could see their dusky forms among the lower branches, with vast numbers of bees flying about them, whose presence they seemed almost to disregard.

The two natives were so busily employed that they did not at first perceive us; but when they came down, they regarded us with much astonishment, and we were afraid that they would turn tail and run off, without giving us the honey which it was our object to obtain. We therefore made all the friendly signs we could think of, and I having fortunately a gaily printed cotton handkerchief in my pocket, presented it to them, signifying at the same time that we wished some of the honey in return.

Our quiet manner quickly disarmed their suspicions, and returning with us, they poured out as much honey as our two tin pots could contain.

I may as well describe the mode of finding the honey the bee-hunters adopt. On perceiving a bee sucking the juice from flowers, he hurries to the nearest pool and selects a spot where the banks shelve gradually. He then lying on his face fills his mouth with water, and patiently awaits the arrival of the bee: as the insect requires moisture, he knows that ere long it will come and drink. The moment it approaches him he blows the water from his mouth over it, thus slightly stunning it. Before it has recovered, he seizes it and by means of some gum fastens to its legs a tuft of white down, which he has obtained from the neighbouring trees. The insect flies in a straight line towards its nest, while the white down serving to impede the progress, enables the hunter to keep it in view, till it reaches its home.

We ate the honey with a small supply of biscuit, and found it far more satisfactory food than the tough parrots had proved.

Having taken a last drink and filled up our water-bottles, we parted on friendly terms with the natives; when, saddling our horses, we continued our journey.

"There is little chance of our reaching another river with more water in it than the last, to camp by," observed my brother; "I see none marked down on the maps for leagues ahead."

We passed through the same sort of scenery as before, with the same dreary views on either side, so that we might have fancied that we had already crossed the country a dozen times.

We at length came to the bed of a stream, no longer however containing water, though I doubt not that we should have obtained it by digging beneath the surface.

The appearance of the bee-hunters had warned us that there were natives about, and we had been cautioned against trusting them. We heard that they had at different times murdered a number of unfortunate hut-keepers and shepherds up the country, so that we were inclined to form very unfavourable opinions of the aborigines. Toby, to be sure, was faithful enough, but then he was semi-civilized. We now asked him if he thought that there were many natives in the neighbourhood to whom the bee-hunters belonged.

He shook his head—"May be!" he said; "bad mans, keep out of him way."

This advice we were ready enough to adopt, and we had no fear, should we meet them on the open ground, of keeping them at bay; but we wished especially to avoid being caught asleep, either at night or resting during the noon-day heat.

We had, at this time, literally no experience about Australia. We had read a few books, to be sure, but Mr. Strong had not described the country, and only advised our father to send us out without incumbrances of any description—a small stock of serviceable clothes, a few books and a box of pills apiece. We followed out his injunctions almost to the letter, adding only some well-made tools, a fowling-piece each, and a supply of ammunition, to which we added on our arrival a few necessaries for travelling in the bush.

Thus we found that one animal could carry all our worldly possessions, a few odd articles for immediate use being packed in our saddle-bags. We were now, as the day was wearing on, looking out for a convenient place to camp. We tried to make Toby understand that we wished for one in which we could not easily be surprised by natives, or if surprised, where we could defend ourselves with some hope of success.

The nature of the ground had changed since the morning, and we now entered a rocky and wild-looking district.

Here we should have no difficulty, we thought, in selecting a spot for our camp. We were looking about, when we spied in the distance what appeared to be the figure of a man standing against a tree. My brother instantly rode forward and I following him saw a person who, to all appearance, though in bush costume, was a gentleman, bound with his hands behind his back, and secured firmly to a tree. He was deadly pale and seemed so much exhausted that he did not even speak to us as we approached.

To leap from our horses and release him without asking questions, was the work of a minute. Having put him on his feet and waited until he had somewhat recovered, we inquired how he had been placed in the position in which we had found him.

"Some rascally bushrangers surprised, and 'stuck me up,'" he answered. "I had just dismounted, when three of them, who had been lying in ambush, suddenly sprang on me, and before I could draw my revolver, knocked me down.

"I fully believed that they intended to murder me, but they contented themselves with carrying off my horse and arms and ammunition and everything I had about me; having lashed me to this tree, and then golloped away, leaving me to the chance of dying of thirst and starvation, or being gnawed to death by the dingoes. Had you not come up, such might have been my fate; and, believe me, I am deeply grateful to you for rescuing me from it."

We had been aware of the possibility that we might meet with natives, but had not thought of the likelihood of encountering bushrangers, indeed we fancied that the country was no longer infested by such characters.

We, of course, having assured the stranger that we were very glad to have been of use to him, invited him to accompany us until he could obtain another horse, and offered to let him ride one of ours by turns.

"I should like however to try and catch the fellows who robbed you;" exclaimed Guy. "Is there any chance of overtaking them? Surely they will encamp not far from this, and if we follow their tracks we might come upon them as suddenly as they surprised you."

"Very little chance of that," observed the stranger. "They are desperate fellows, and, knowing that every man's hand is against them, keep a strict watch. They are aware that it is possible that I might be released, and will probably ere this have got a good many miles away. I am, however, grateful to you for your offer, though I am sorry to delay you. I confess that, without a gun or flint and steel, I should be very sorry to perform the rest of the journey on foot by myself. I am going to the north-west, and I judge, from the direction you were riding, that our roads lie the same way."

Guy told him that we were bound for Mr. Strong's station, which we understood was nearly a hundred

"SOME RASCALLY BUSHRANGERS 'STUCK ME UP.'" [*p.* 11

miles off; and at the rate we could travel with our baggage horse, we did not expect to reach it for three or four days.

Observing how ill the stranger looked I suggested that we should at once look out a good spot for camping.

"I can help you, as I know the country," said the stranger. "A short distance further on there is a water-hole in what during the rainy season is sometimes a torrent; we can there obtain all the requisites for a camp."

I now insisted that he should mount my horse, and we set out.

Pushing forward, we soon reached the spot he spoke of. Our new companion, after examining the ground, told us that the bushrangers had been there, and after watering their horses had ridden on, as he supposed they would, and that we need have no apprehensions of an attack from them.

We soon hobbled the horses in the usual fashion, fastening their legs together with leathern straps in such a way as to make it impossible for them to move beyond a slow walk, so that if they were inclined to stray they could not go far.

Toby quickly lighted a fire, while the stranger by our advice rested near it. Guy and I taking our guns went out in different directions in search of game, which is usually to be found near a water-hole in Australia. We soon came back, Guy with a brace of pigeons and I with three parrots, so that we had ample food for all hands. As we had damper and tea, we enjoyed a satisfactory meal which greatly revived our new friend. While we were seated round the fire—Toby watching the horses—the stranger inquired if we were related to Mr. Strong. This led us to give him a brief sketch of our history.

"May I ask your name?" he said. "Mine is Norman Bracewell."

"And ours is Thurston," said my brother.

"What! Guy Thurston?" exclaimed Bracewell, leaning forward and grasping Guy's hand; "I thought from the first that I knew your features. We were at school together. 'Little Guy' we used to call you, and you haven't forgotten me?"

"No indeed!" said Guy warmly, "you always stood my friend when the big fellows tried to bully me, and I have a perfect recollection of your countenance. I have often wished to know what had become of you, but could only hear that you had gone abroad."

"I thought of writing to let you know, in case you should ever come out to Australia; but I fancied that that was so unlikely and the chances of meeting you so small that I did not carry out my intention. You must stop at my hut. The longer you stay the better. We will have many a talk about old times and I think I can put you up to all sorts of information which will be useful to you in the country. To tell you the truth, I doubt if you will find your cousin, Mr. Strong, as I heard that he had gone northwards to occupy a new station, some hundreds of miles off, and if so you will probably find no one to give you a welcome at his house except some old hut-keeper.

On hearing this, Guy and I gladly agreed to stop a few days with Bracewell until we could obtain some definite information as to the movements of our cousin.

We told him of our meeting with the two bee-hunters.

"This proves that there are some natives in the neighbourhood. They may be honest, but they may also be ill-disposed, as are many of the blacks in this region. I advise that we keep a strict watch at night, and I offer to stand guard part of the time," observed Bracewell.

We agreed to keep a watch, but after the trying time he had gone through we thought that he ought to have a quiet night's rest so as to be the better able to continue his journey the next morning.

Toby had put up a rough hut of boughs, which would afford two of us at a time sufficient shelter from the night air. Of rain there was no fear. Toby erected a hut for himself with a few boughs stuck upright in the ground, which formed all the protection he required.

I undertook to keep the first watch, and I promised my brother that I would call him when I could no longer remain with my eyes open. From past experience we knew that it would not do to trust Toby, who would be very certain to be down as soon as he found that our eyes were off him. Guy and Bracewell were quickly asleep and I commenced walking to and fro, keeping a look-out on every side and sometimes stopping to throw a few sticks on the fire. I could see the horses safely feeding near at hand,

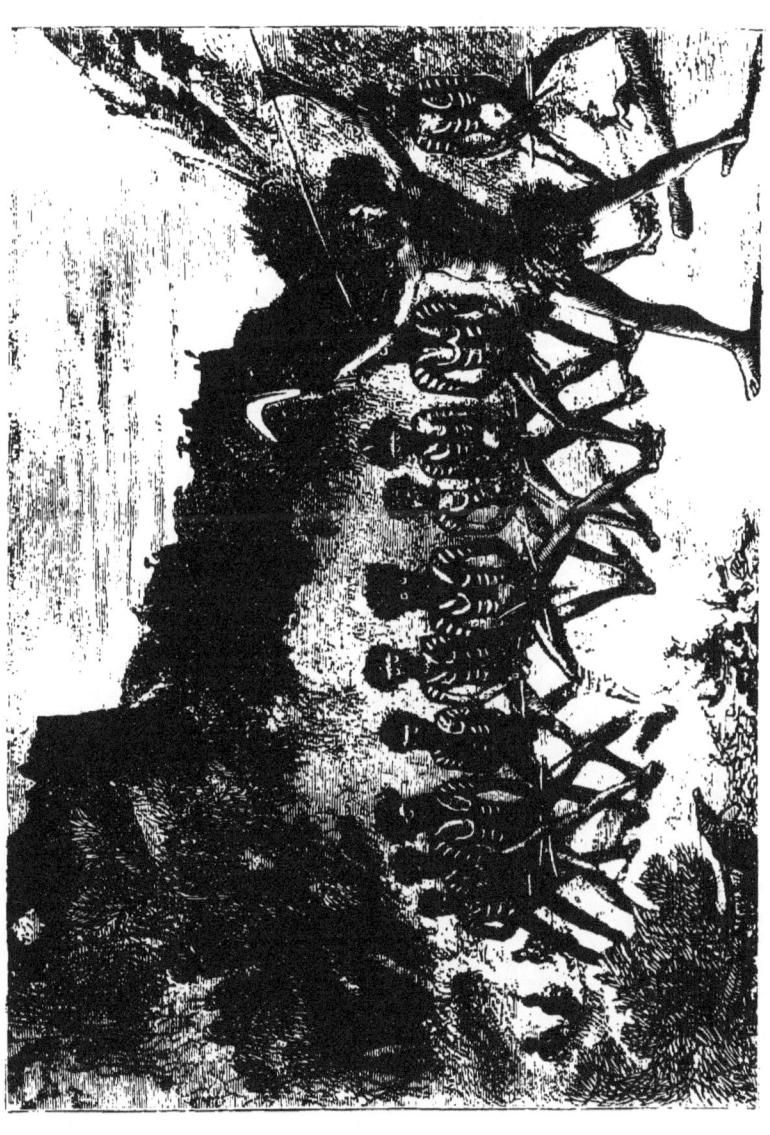

A NATIVE DANCE.

and so perfect was the silence which reigned around that I could not fancy that there was any real necessity for keeping awake. Still, as I had undertaken to do so, I should not have felt justified in lying down. I should probably have let the fire out, and the smoke from that was at all events useful to keep mosquitoes and sandflies somewhat at bay. Should the fire go out it was no more than possible that a pack of dingoes might creep up, and while we were in darkness drive the horses away, or carry off our saddle bags, or tear our saddles and sleeping-rugs to pieces. I persevered therefore, stopping every now and then to amuse myself by looking up at the starlighted sky and trying to make out the various constellations, conspicuous among which was the brilliant cross of the southern hemisphere. Except the occasional croak of a frog, the cry of a night bird, or the chirp of a cricket, not a sound had reached my ears; when suddenly, as I was watching the moon rising above the rocks on one side of the camp, the most unearthly shrieks and yells rent the air. Guy, awakening, started to his feet.

"What's the matter?" he exclaimed. "I dreamed that savages were upon us, and expected the next moment to have a spear through me."

"I haven't seen any savages, but those sounds seem scarcely human, I wonder Bracewell hasn't been awakened by them. We must rouse up Toby and learn what he thinks they are."

The fearful noise still continued. We stood with our arms ready expecting every moment to see a herd of savages rush in upon us, for that the sounds were produced by natives we could have no doubt. We quickly made Toby spring to his feet.

"What's all that noise about?" asked Guy.

"He-he-he, ho-ho-ho! dat corrobboree," answered Toby who did not appear, as we expected would be the case, at all astonished at the uproar.

Bracewell at length awoke and confirmed what Toby had said, that the savages were indulging in one of their native dances.

"I should like to go and see it," I exclaimed; "can we do so without risk of being discovered?"

Taking Toby to guide us, while Bracewell remained in camp, we set out. We were scarcely prepared for the strange and weird sight which we saw as we looked over some low bushes we had just reached. Before us was an open glade, beyond which the moon was rising brightly. In the centre of the glade burned a fire. Seated on the ground were a number of figures rattling sticks together. Suddenly there burst forth out of the darkness a score of skeleton-like figures who threw themselves into every possible attitude, now stretching out their legs, now springing up and clapping their hands, and all the time shrieking, laughing and singing, and following a big black fellow who acted as fugleman and stood on one side with stick in hand to direct the proceedings.

Not for a moment did they cease, though every now and then we might have fancied that they had disappeared had we not distinguished their black backs turned towards us. We watched until we grew weary of the sight, but the dancers appeared in no way tired; and as we saw no chance of their giving in, we retreated to our own camp, pretty well tired out and assured that they would not molest us during the night.

CHAPTER II.

The night passed as Bracewell had predicted, without a visit from the natives; and as he assured us that they were not at all likely to attack four armed men in the day-time, we, being anxious to become better acquainted with them, agreed before setting off to pay a visit to their camp. They were sure indeed to find ours out; so that it would be as well to show that we had no fear of them, and to gain their friendship. On examining the birds we had cooked the previous evening we found they had been nearly devoured by the white ants, a large nest of which we discovered a short distance from the camp. We had therefore to look out for some fresh provisions. Bracewell was a much better shot than either of us; and, taking my gun, in a few minutes he killed a small kangaroo which he found as it was about to spring out of the bush where it had spent the night, scarcely a hundred yards from the camp. Having skinned it in the most scientific fashion, the joints were put on to roast. We had now an abundance for our noon-day meal; for, as the animal was about four feet long, including the tail which was nearly half its length, it afforded us a good supply of meat.

We should have preferred starting at daybreak, but without food we none of us felt inclined to commence our journey. Toby indeed gave us to understand that he could not think of leaving while so much good meat remained to be eaten. Having given him as much as we all three consumed, we packed up the remainder in our saddle-bags and then—I insisting that Bracewell should mount my horse while I walked—we set off for the native village which we caught sight of a short distance to the north of our camp. The inhabitants were lying about in front of it, evidently enjoying the *otium cum dignitate*. The men mostly stretched on the ground surrounded by their dogs, while the women were squatting outside their leafy bowers. The huts, if so they can be called, were placed in a semi-circle, and were formed by thick boughs stuck in the ground joining at the top on which other boughs were lightly thrown. They were scarcely more than four feet in height and might be described rather as screens than huts, as their only object appeared to be to keep off the wind from the inhabitants and the small fires which burnt before them. On the outside were stuck their spears ready for instant use. Except some pieces of opossum skin round their loins, the men wore no garments, though several of them had fillets bound round their brows. Two or three were smoking short clay pipes obtained from shepherds or hut-keepers with whom they had come in contact. Several of the men started up, and seizing their spears advanced as they saw us approach, but the greater number lay gorged with food on the ground, not apparently noticing us. Bracewell, who could speak Toby's lingo, told him to say to the black fellows, that we wished to be their friends; that their carrobboree had afforded us a good deal of amusement; and that if we could kill a kangaroo we would give it to them to make another feast the next night.

As soon as Toby had translated what had been said, the blacks began chattering away in the most extraordinary fashion.

As they ceased Toby informed us that they were highly pleased with our offer. They wished to remain friends with the white men, and if we chose to stop with them we should be welcome. Of course, we had no inclination to do this, but we asked if two or three of them would accompany us to carry home any game we might kill. They however declined the invitation, saying that they were well filled already, of which fact their distended condition was sufficient evidence.

"Well then, as we cannot turn back, you will have to go without a kangaroo, even though we may shoot one," said Bracewell, and telling Toby to wish them a friendly farewell we rode on.

As I was very active and had been accustomed to running at school, I easily kept up with the horses. At length however, as the sun grew hotter, I should have been glad enough to remount. Bracewell, observing that I was becoming fatigued, insisted on getting off his horse, but of this I would not hear. He however dismounted, when Guy made him get on again and put me on his own horse. Before long,

THE ROCK KANGAROO.

however, my brother was nearly knocked up, and seeing this I proposed that he should remount, and that I should ride Toby's horse. Toby made a wry face, for, although better able to run than any of us, he considered that it was more dignified to ride.

As we rode along we kept a look out for kangaroos, as we should have been glad to kill one for ourselves, although our black friends were not likely to benefit by it.

We had gone some way when we caught sight of a dark object appearing just above a thick mass of leaves some two hundred yards away. Standing up in my stirrups I saw that it was the head of a kangaroo who was engaged in pulling off the foliage. I called to Bracewell and my brother, hoping that if we could get nearer before the creature moved away, we might shoot it.

Throwing the halter of the baggage-horse, which I had been leading, to Toby, I rode towards the spot, unslinging my rifle and as I did so ramming down a ball. The creature was more wide-awake than I had supposed. I had just got near enough to fire, when it broke from its cover in fine style and, after taking a few jumps to see in what direction to go, it started forward over the open ground without apparent effort.

"That's a large *boomer*, an old one!" shouted Bracewell, "he'll give us a long run. If we had dogs we should soon however catch him."

In the excitement of the chase, forgetting that we ran great risk of knocking up our horses, away we started. Although the animal had only two legs to run on and had an enormous tail to carry, which does not, I really believe, help it, though it serves to balance itself in its upright position, so far did it get ahead of us that it was useless firing. I had scarcely noticed the direction it was taking, but on looking round I found that it was leading us back to the spot from which we had come. How far it had got I cannot say, when four or five black fellows started up with spears in their hands uttering loud shouts and shrieks. The *boomer* saw that it had no chance of escape in that direction, being perhaps better acquainted with its black enemies than with the strange creatures on four legs which had been pursuing it. It therefore stopped and gave us time to approach before it bounded round and made off to the right. I had thrown myself from my horse, for I had no notion at that time of firing from my saddle. I took a steady aim and pulled the trigger. My bullet must have hit it on the hinder leg, for it slackened its pace. In the meantime Bracewell and Guy dashed forward. The creature, instead of continuing its flight, again stopped, and facing the horsemen as they approached struck out with one of its hinder claws, and had not Bracewell suddenly turned his steed, so furiously did it strike that he would have been severely wounded. Turning round however he dealt it so heavy a blow on the head with his riding whip that it staggered, and Guy firing brought it to the ground. The natives, whom we recognised as our friends of the morning, now came up and claimed the prize. Bracewell gave them to understand that we must first cut out as many steaks

A NATIVE VILLAGE.

as we required. When this was done we handed the body over to them. They appeared highly delighted and especially struck by the moderate quantity we claimed. We had now to turn back to where we had left Toby in charge of the baggage animal. I had some secret apprehensions that, if not honest, he might bolt with our traps and be received with open arms as a wealthy man among some of his countrymen. I was not aware at the time that he belonged to a tribe regarded as hereditary enemies by the people inhabiting the country we were travelling through, and that he was as likely to lose his life at their hands as any white man would be. We looked about in all directions and at length, to our no small satisfaction, espied him still standing by the horses and wondering what had become of us. We had lost considerable time by our hunting, though we had obtained a good dinner, and of course had been delayed also by one of the party having to proceed on foot.

While we were seated round our camp-fire Bracewell said—

"I scarcely like to make the proposal I am about to do, and yet perhaps you will not object. If you will consent to remain in camp here and allow me to take one of your horses, I will ride forward and bring a couple of fresh ones from my station. Should you not do this I must insist on walking, though I shall of necessity delay you. I confess also, that I am anxious to give notice that the bushrangers are abroad, or they may be visiting my hut or some of my neighbours, and carry off arms and ammunition, which is chiefly what they come after, for they don't find much else than food in the shepherds' huts."

"Pray do as you think best," said Guy, "I am sure Maurice will agree with me that we should not at all mind remaining stationary for a few hours, nor will our other horses, which require rest."

I thought the plan a good one, and before the day had actually broken, Bracewell mounted my horse and away he rode at a rate which assured us that we should not be long alone. As Toby had plenty of food, he did not grumble at the delay, but sat himself down contentedly at the fire which he promised to keep alight, while we took our guns and went to shoot some birds or a kangaroo if we could see one.

The great drawback to a traveller in a hot country is the impossibility of preserving fresh meat, which exposed to the sun quickly becomes uneatable. What we killed one day was therefore unfit for food the next, and we had each morning to shoot some more game, or content ourselves with damper and tea.

We had already become pretty skilful in baking damper, which consists simply of flour and water, kneaded on a board, and baked in the form of a large biscuit under the ashes.

We saw several kangaroos, but they bounded away before we could get near enough to shoot them, and had to content ourselves as before with a couple of parrots and as many pigeons, which was an ample supply, for although the over-high kangaroo meat did not suit our palates, Toby had no objection to it.

We had been shooting for some time, and were

making our way back to camp, when we caught sight in the distance of three horsemen, their heads and those of their steeds, occasionally appearing above the brushwood. They appeared to be coming towards us.

At first we thought that they must be Bracewell and two companions; but as we could make out no led horses, and they were not approaching from the direction he would appear, we concluded that they must be strangers.

"What if they should be bushrangers?" said Guy. "If they catch Toby alone they are certain to carry off our baggage and horses, and will probably shoot him to prevent him giving information."

"The sooner we get back to camp the better," I answered.

We hurried on, keeping ourselves concealed as much as possible. "It would be prudent to load our guns with ball," said Guy; "the fellows won't know that we suspect them, and may think that they can stick us up with perfect ease."

Fortunately our horses were close to the camp, and as soon as we reached it we sent Toby to bring them in, not telling him that we suspected the character of the strangers. As they approached we anxiously examined their appearance, which was certainly not in their favour. They were savage-looking fellows with long beards, their unkempt hair hanging over their shoulders. They pulled up suddenly when they saw us standing with our backs to a couple of large trees, our baggage and saddles piled on the ground, and Toby holding our horses.

"What is your pleasure, friends?" asked Guy. The fellows examined us without answering.

"You look as if you'd know us again should we come across you," said Guy. "Just take my advice. Ride on and leave us to cook our dinner."

"Who are you, young chaps, and where are you going?" inquired one of the horsemen, who from his appearance we concluded was the leader of the party.

"We are going our own way and are not inclined to give that information to those who have no authority to ask it," replied Guy in a firm voice.

"Did you fall in with a young fellow who had been stuck up by bushrangers?" inquired the man.

The question convinced us that we were not mistaken as to the character of our visitors.

"I have just told you that we are not going to answer any questions from those who have no right to put them," said Guy.

"Oh, oh, oh!" cried the man, making a movement as if he was about to unsling his gun.

"If you do that, I'll fire," shouted Guy. "Our rifles are loaded with ball; now ride on, we do not wish to take your lives, but we have no intention of being stuck up."

During this conversation I was looking at the other two fellows, who had not spoken but seemed to be waiting until their chief gave a sign to them to act. As my eye ranged over the countenance of one of them, it struck me forcibly that I had seen the man before, but when or where, I could not recollect. He was evidently very young, for while the faces of the others were covered with hair, he had but a small moustache on his lips, but exposure to the hot sun had so tanned his complexion, that had he been an intimate friend I might have failed to recognise him. He looked at me and then at my brother, whose attention was occupied by the older bushranger and did not notice him as I was doing.

"Oh, oh, oh!" exclaimed the man, after the warning Guy had given him; and, without saying another word, he and his companions turned their horses' heads and rode away in the direction from whence they had come. Probably they had been attracted by the smoke of our fire, and expected to find some travellers unprepared for them; so we should have been had we not fallen in with Bracewell, and should certainly have lost our baggage and horses, and perhaps our lives.

"We have had a narrow escape, for there is no doubt about those fellows being bushrangers," I observed to Guy.

"Not the slightest," replied my brother. "I felt that there was only one way to deal with them. Had we shown the slightest hesitation or nervousness, they would have attempted to frighten us into submission."

"Did you notice the countenance of one of the others?" I asked. "I could not help fancying that I knew it well. If it were not so very improbable, I should say that it was that of a fellow I remember at school when I first went there. I wish that you had observed him, for as you must have known him better than I did, you would have been more sure about the matter."

"What, do you mean the youngest of the three?" asked Guy. "The fact is I did note him. It struck me that he was wonderfully like a fellow I always stood clear of, though he especially tried to make friends with me. If you remember the name of the person you think he was, tell me, and I shall better be able to judge whether I am right."

"I am nearly certain then that it was Cyril Vinson."

"You are right," answered Guy. "He was a clever fellow without a particle of principle; and I remember hearing it reported some time after he left school, that he had committed forgery, and that, although he was not convicted, his friends had sent him out of the country."

We talked over the matter, and agreed that it was very strange we should so soon after our arrival in the country have fallen in, under such extraordinary circumstances, with two old school-fellows.

The day passed by without another visit, either from the bushrangers or the blacks. As may be supposed, we kept a remarkably bright look out during the night. Either Guy or I remained awake, walking up and down in the neighbourhood of our camp-fire. Directly the bells on the necks of our horses sounded faint, we sent out Toby to drive them in, that we might run as little risk as possible of their being carried off.

Bracewell had told us that sometimes natives stole up and speared the horses at night, or tried to drive them away from the camp, though they might not venture to attack their owners. We had chiefly

THE KANGAROO.

therefore to fear a trick of this sort being played us, but it was almost impossible to guard against the horses being surprised during the darkness, should they be at any distance from the camp.

As those we had fallen in with appeared to be friendly, we hoped that we should escape so unpleasant a loss.

As the next day passed on we looked at our watches, anxiously expecting Bracewell. With the chance of another visit from the bushrangers, we did not like to go far from the camp; but we shot as many birds as we wanted, though Toby would have been happier had we brought him a kangaroo, that he might gorge himself to his heart's content.

As I had been awake so much during the night, I felt very sleepy, and had thrown myself on the ground to get some rest, when I heard Guy say—

"Here come a couple of horsemen, but whether they are Bracewell and a companion, or the bushrangers returning, I cannot say. At all events we must be prepared for them."

I sprang to my feet, and Toby was sent to bring in the horses. Our apprehensions of another visit from the bushrangers were soon set at rest when we recognized Bracewell, who was followed by another man leading a spare horse.

"I am sorry to have kept you so long," he exclaimed, as he threw himself from his steed. "Our horses had strayed, frightened by the blacks, who have killed one of them. If we come across the fellows they must look out for broken heads in consequence. However, Bob and I succeeded in catching three, and then lost no time in coming to you."

When we told him of the visit we had received from the bushrangers, he exclaimed—

"We must run those fellows down. It is too bad that we should be unable to ride in security through the country without the risk of being robbed, perhaps murdered, by such villains."

We immediately saddled our horses, packed our traps on our baggage animal, and prepared to go forward under Bracewell's guidance. Old Bob, his hut-keeper and factotum, dropped behind to drive on the baggage horse at a greater speed than Toby was inclined to move. I heard him talking to the black in a lingo which was utterly incomprehensible to me.

Bracewell was much astonished when Guy told him that we had recognized Cyril Vinson among the bushrangers. We were once more, on account of the slow pace of our baggage horse, compelled to camp, but as Bracewell wished to get back to his hut that night, he rode forward, leaving old Bob to guide us in the morning. Old Bob undertook to keep watch, and as he did not look like a man who would go to sleep while so engaged, we were able to rest securely.

It was nearly evening the next day when we caught sight of the huts forming our friend's station. He came forward to meet us.

"I expected you somewhat sooner," he said. "As Bob was away, I was engaged in performing one of his duties—feeding the inhabitants of my farm-yard. I have a curious lot, which I have caught and tamed

"FEEDING THE INHABITANTS OF MY FARM-YARD." [p. 40.

at different times. Here they are, come and have a look at them."

And he led the way to an enclosure with a hut on one side of it. As he stooped down, ducks and fowls rushed forward to obtain the food he held in his hand, the pigs came grunting up, and several long-legged birds—storks I believe they were—stood by waiting for their share, numerous parrots and parroquets were perched on the railings, as tame as the barn-door fowls, while a laughing jackass looked on complacently from an overhanging bough, every now and then uttering its strange notes.

Bracewell directed Bob to finish feeding the birds, and ushered us into the hut. It was about thirty feet long and twelve wide, roughly built with a verandah in front, and contained a centre room and one on either side. The interior was far neater than I had expected from the appearance of the outside, and was furnished with tables and chairs, and several cupboards and some book-shelves; the walls were ornamented with a few pictures and native weapons, while two spare guns and some pistols were against them. A couple of large Scotch deer hounds of a badger-like colour accompanied their master. They were intelligent, powerful-looking animals, and were used, he told us, for hunting the kangaroo. Before a fire in a smaller hut on one side of the main building, two joints of mutton were roasting.

"I can give you but bush fare," said our host, "mutton, damper, and tea; for of wine and spirits I have none, with the exception of a bottle of brandy, which I keep safely locked up for reasons which I will explain to you."

Besides the large hut I have described there were two smaller ones and a shed, which served as a stable and cowhouse. Near them was an enclosed field and small kitchen-garden, such as is not often seen at an Australian cattle or sheep station. To the west was a thick wood, which afforded shelter from the winds blowing at times hot and sand-laden from the interior; while in front was a slight dip, at the bottom of which was the bed of a river, but through it a trickling stream alone at present found its way to the eastward. Here and there appeared groves of acacias, while as far as the eye could reach in every other direction were grassy downs, scattered over which we caught sight of a considerable herd of sheep wending their way homewards. Altogether, Bracewell's station presented a more civilised aspect than any we had fallen in with on our journey.

CHAPTER III.

WE spent a pleasant evening with Bracewell, talking over old times and our future prospects. He gave us a great deal of good advice, by which we hoped to profit.

"I am very glad you have come out, old fellows, for I am sure you will succeed if you stick to work," he observed. "I have not done badly. I began with eight head of cattle, and now I have three hundred; and with forty sheep, which have become upwards of two thousand. I should have had a larger number had I known more of the business when I commenced, but I have lost many by disease and dingoes, and the natives. You must make up your mind to take the rough and smooth together, and not despair though you happen to get what they call a run of ill-luck—which in nine cases out of ten arises from a man's carelessness. I confess that I have sometimes felt my solitude; but yet, with my friends on the shelves up there, and these faithful animals at my feet, I have had no great reason to complain. I also remember that I should have been much worse off in many respects had I remained at home."

"But what about the blacks and the bushrangers?" asked Guy.

"The blacks have been troublesome at times, but I have hitherto been able to keep them at bay," answered Bracewell; "and with regard to the bushrangers, none have ever paid me a visit. The fellows who stuck me up the other day were the first I had the misfortune to fall in with. I wonder if Vinson recognised me; but I think not, or if he did he kept out of sight. I am grieved to think it was him, as he will certainly, before long, come to an untimely end; for no bushranger ultimately escapes, and most of them run but a very short career: they either get shot or die of starvation and sickness in the bush."

When we talked of continuing our journey the next day, Bracewell would not hear of it.

"Your relative does not expect you, he observed, "and you will pick up more useful knowledge on my station than you will on a more extensive run; besides which I want you to have some hunting with me, to show you this part of the country."

Nothing loth, we agreed to Bracewell's proposal. It was not until a late hour, for the bush, that we turned into our bunks in one of the side-rooms, which he told us he kept as his guest-chamber. Bracewell slept in a hammock in the sitting-room, while old Bob occupied the other room.

The first day we spent riding over the run, visiting the cattle and inspecting the sheep. In the evening Bracewell proposed that we should go into the neighbouring wood in search of opossum, whose skins he wished to obtain to make some rugs, which he said he wanted to sleep on when camping out or to serve as coverlets in cold weather. His shepherd possessed a couple of small dogs, famous opossum hunters. The sheep having been penned, their master was requested to accompany us.

The Australian opossum is a long-bodied short-legged little animal, with a furry tail by which he can suspend himself on the branches of trees, while it assists him to make rapid progress among them. He is fond of hiding himself in the holes of decayed trees, out of which it is no easy matter to smoke him. Being a nocturnal animal he is more generally captured during the day-time, for the bright light of the sun puzzles him and he knows not in what direction to make his escape.

We soon arrived at a large hole in a gum-tree round which the dogs began barking, leaving us no doubt that several opossums were ensconced within. Our first care was to collect a quantity of sticks and green leaves; when, a fire being kindled inside the hole, the smoke began to ascend, filling the whole of the cavity, which extended to where the boughs branched off. The moon having risen, we could see almost as well as in day-light. Before long, three or four little creatures emerged from the hole and began to make their way upwards. One, however, almost suffocated by the smoke, fell to the ground; when the dogs, instantly pouncing upon it, would have torn it to pieces had not their master pulled them off. Guy shot another, and two more were brought to the ground by the sticks which the rest of us hove at them before they had recovered their senses, after having been so unexpectedly smoked out of their nests.

We were equally successful with two other trees, round which the dogs gave tongue, and after an hour's hunting we returned carrying our prizes, which took Bracewell and his shepherd some time to clean.

"Of course opussum hunting is but tame work, I'll allow," exclaimed Bracewell while washing his hands after having cleaned the last of the beasts; "but as you are both good horsemen and have steady nerves we will to-morrow go in chase of some wild cattle which have appeared in the bush not far off. I should not object to kill a couple of them, as we are in want of fresh meat and I cannot afford to slaughter my sheep. Perhaps on the way we may fall in with a kangaroo, which is sure to give us good sport."

Next morning found us all three galloping along through the open forest. We trusted entirely to Bracewell's guidance, for before we had gone a mile, I confess I should have had a difficulty in finding my way back again.

"We are in luck," cried Bracewell, as in less than half an hour we caught sight of four head of the wild cattle we were in search of. As we approached they began pawing on the ground, sticking out their tails and looking anything but amiable.

"They will charge if we don't take care," observed Bracewell. "Shout and crack your whips, that will make them show us their flanks."

We had, I should have said, our guns in readiness, and a brace of pistols in our belts, so that we were

OPOSSUM HUNTING. [p. 47.

well armed for the encounter with a wild bull, who, looking upon human beings and every other animal as enemies, was a dangerous character to engage.

Bracewell had before instructed us how to act under such ordinary circumstances as were likely to occur. The cracking of our whips, and our loud shouts, at length frightened the three bulls, and instead of running at us they turned tail and off they went.

"Tally-ho!" shouted Bracewell, and we made chase.

Our object was now to overtake them. Bracewell having got up to a powerful red bull, for a few seconds he and the animal kept time together; then gaining a little and keeping it on his right side he fired, and the superb beast, with a low bellow, crashed headlong to the ground. Pulling up for a moment he galloped after me, as I dashed on close to another bull I had singled out; but in consequence of a fallen tree which would have compelled me to slacken speed, I had ranged up on the wrong side, so that I could not fire with due effect. Fearing however that the bull would escape, I took the best aim I could, fired, and wounded it. The bull, maddened with rage, charged wildly at my horse.

"Spur for your life," shouted Bracewell. I did so, for I expected every moment to see the bull rip open my steed with his powerful horns, and I knew that if it was gored I might be trampled to death.

The bull came thundering behind me and actually touched my horse, which nearly sent me over its head as it kicked out viciously to defend itself. Happily

Bracewell was close behind, and coming up presented the muzzle of his pistol at the bull's head. The next moment I was safe. In the meantime Guy had been pursuing a third bull. I had heard him fire twice. I now saw the animal rushing on, with head down, about to run at him. Fortunately a tree was near at hand, round which he managed to guide his horse, when the bull for a moment losing sight of him he was able to take a steady aim: he fired and the monster rolled over.

"Nervous work!" exclaimed Bracewell. "You fellows have behaved capitally, though I really forgot the danger to which you might be exposed, but I am very thankful that no harm has been done. We'll now ride back as hard as we can go, and get the cart to bring in the meat before the dingoes or black fellows or the ants have taken possession of it."

We agreed that hunting wild cattle was more exciting sport than galloping after kangaroos, although we fancied that the latter was the finest amusement to be found in Australia. Not a moment was lost on our arrival at home in getting the cart under way, and Guy and I undertook to accompany it, but Bracewell could not again leave the station during the time that old Bob who drove it, and Toby who went to assist him, were away. As we approached the scene of action, we caught sight of a number of what at a distance I should have fancied were ordinary dogs—with sharp muzzles, short, erect ears, and bushy tails—hovering round the spot.

"They're dingoes!" cried Guy. "The rascals have already commenced operations on one of the bulls.

We must drive them off or old Bob won't have much meat to carry home."

We dashed at the brutes with our riding whips, which we brought into active play. Some well-aimed lashes on their backs made the dingoes turn tail and retreat to a safe distance, where they stood watching the operation of cutting up one of the animals.

While we were assisting Bob and Toby to load the cart with the flesh of the first bullock, the dingoes made a sudden dash at the carcase of the animal on which they had before commenced.

This was more than we could stand.

"If I was you, sir, I'd give them a lesson they'll not forget," cried Bob; and throwing ourselves on our horses, we rode at the savage pack, using the butts of our whips with such good effect that we knocked over upwards of half a dozen before the rest of the pack took to flight. To prevent their returning, we pursued them as they went off in the direction of the station, when, firing our pistols, we brought down two or three more; but we were soon thrown behind by having to pull up and reload, and the pack, keeping wonderfully well together, again managed to distance us. Still, excited by the chase, we kept on, the dead dingoes marking the course we had taken. Our horses, having been somewhat tired by the chase after the wild cattle and the rides to and from the station, did not make as good play as they might otherwise have done. Neither Guy nor I thought of pulling up, however, while we had the chance of killing more of the brutes. At last my horse, stumbling, threw me over his head, and I lost the rein; when finding himself at liberty, away he galloped, showing no inclination to be caught. I shouted to my brother, who had got some distance on; he heard me, and seeing what had occurred went in chase of my steed, which by occasionally doubling and then galloping off again, well nigh tired out his horse. I ran here and there hoping to catch the animal, but it took good care to avoid me. At length however Guy got hold of it, by which time, of course, the pack had escaped. We now had to consider what road we should take, but when we looked round we found it was a question difficult to decide.

"If we could but come across one of the dead dingoes, we could easily make our way back to where we left old Bob," observed Guy.

We felt sure that the last dingo we had killed could not be far off.

"This is the spot where my horse threw me, and I had just before knocked over a dingo," I said, "I know it by that peculiar-looking gum-tree."

We rode on, expecting to come upon the dead dingo, but though we searched about we could nowhere discover it. On and on we went, still no dingoes could we see, nor could we distinguish the track made by our horses' feet. The sky had become overcast, but though we could not see the sun, we knew that it must be near setting. In a short time the increasing darkness made us feel somewhat uncomfortable about the chance of being benighted.

We cooeyed as loudly as we could in the hope that Bob and Toby would hear our voices, but no answer reached us. Had we been riding horses belonging to the station, we might have let them select their course and they would probably have taken us in; but we had mounted our own beasts, which could not be depended on. Still, as long as there was light sufficient to enable us to avoid knocking our heads against the boughs of trees, we rode on, hoping that we might at length reach the station. At last, however, we agreed that we must make up our minds to spend the night in the bush, hungry and thirsty as we felt. Next morning we thought we should, at all events, easily find our way. We accordingly dismounted, hobbled our horses, collected materials for a fire, and choosing a spot free from grass we soon kindled a flame, though it rather mocked us as we had nothing to cook at it. We settled that one should keep watch and look after the horses. The poor animals were suffering from thirst as much as we were, and were continually moving away to look for water, for without it they showed little inclination to crop the grass. Had we thought it prudent for both of us to sleep, the night would have appeared to pass by much more quickly than it did. I was very thankful when at length day broke, and we were saluted by the merry call of the laughing jackass. We did not shoot him, but we killed a couple of parrots, which we quickly roasted to satisfy the gnawings of hunger, and then mounting our horses made, as we thought, in the direction of the station. We felt especially vexed with ourselves for losing our way, and causing Bracewell the anxiety he would naturally feel on our account, though he would guess pretty clearly what had happened from the report old Bob would give him on his return.

We had gone some distance, when we caught sight of a fire and a column of smoke rising in the morning air.

"Perhaps that is the camp of some people Bracewell has sent out to look for us," said I.

"It may be that of bushrangers," observed Guy. "It will be prudent, at all events, to approach it cautiously."

Riding on, we caught sight of a black figure with his back towards us, seated before a small fire at which he was apparently engaged in cooking something. His attention absorbed in his occupation, he did not observe us. The delicate morsel he was preparing for his meal was, we afterwards discovered, a large snake. When his ear at length caught the sound of horses' feet, he started up, and seizing the half-roasted snake, scampered off. Had we not made signs to him that we wished to be friends, he would soon have been out of sight. Seeing, however, that we did not unsling our rifles, he gained courage and returned to the fire.

We beckoned to him to continue roasting his snake, and then endeavoured to make him understand that we wanted a guide to conduct us to the station. He seemed determined not to understand our wishes. However, we waited patiently, hoping that when he had eaten his snake he might be more inclined to act as our guide. Finding that we had no intention of molesting him, he took things leisurely. The snake being roasted, he began to stow it away.

"I wonder he doesn't offer us some, though I'm not inclined to eat it," I observed.

"He is a perfect savage, and has no wish to part with his dainty fare," replied Guy.

We thought that the fellow would soon come to an end of the meal, and that then he would pack up the rest of the snake and carry it with him. To our surprise he did not stop until he had swallowed the whole of it, and when we again made signs to him that we wanted him to guide us, he stroked his stomach and signified that he should prefer sleeping by the side of his fire.

Guy at length, losing patience, gave a flourish with his stock whip, when an idea seemed suddenly to strike the black, and getting up he made signs to us to follow him. We naturally supposed that he intended to lead us to the station, and rode after him without hesitation. We had not gone far, however, when a cooee reached our ears. We replied, and presently, looking round in the direction from whence the sound came, we saw Bracewell galloping towards us, followed by Toby.

"I am thankful that I found you sooner than I expected," he said. "Where do you think you were going?"

"To the station," answered Guy.

"You were riding, however, in an opposite direction," said our friend.

"The black we fell in with, undertook to guide us," I remarked.

"The rascal had no intention of taking you to my station. He would probably have led you into the

"SEATED BEFORE A SMALL FIRE, ENGAGED IN COOKING." [*p.* 55.

midst of a gang of his own people who, I have had notice, are encamped in the neighbourhood, and had they found you unprepared they might have speared you for the sake of your horses and clothes. The fellow you fell in with was probably one of their scouts who had been sent forward to ascertain what we were about. Should they have found us off our guard, they might have robbed the huts and carried off some of our cattle and sheep."

While Bracewell was speaking, I looked round and found that the black fellow had disappeared. This strongly corroborated the account our friend had given us.

As we were suffering greatly from thirst, we were anxious to get back as soon as possible. We had, we found, gone at least ten miles out of our way. Bracewell had, however, with the aid of Toby, traced us. Though our horses were tired, their eagerness to obtain water made them exert themselves, and they did not take long to cover the ground. Most thankful we were when we reached the stream close to the station, where we and they could take a good draught of the refreshing fluid.

We then, by our friend's advice—while old Bob was preparing dinner—turned into our bunks and managed to get a sound snooze, awaking much refreshed.

Next morning we had completely recovered from the fatigues we had gone through, and we now felt that we ought to continue our journey to Mr. Strong's.

"But I don't like you two fellows, with only Toby,

to travel through the bush, with a chance of falling in with hostile blacks or those rascally bushrangers, who would only be too glad to stick you up and revenge themselves for your setting me free," said Bracewell. "I have given notice to the police that the latter gentlemen are abroad, and before long, clever as they may think themselves, they will be run to earth; but the blacks are far more difficult customers to deal with—they are here, there, and everywhere. One only knows where they have been when the cattle are found speared, or the hut-keeper murdered, or the sheep driven off. I should like to accompany you myself, but I cannot at present leave my station. However, if you will wait for a couple of days longer I will ride part of the way with you, and in the meantime we will try to ascertain the whereabouts of the mob of blacks, and I shall be able to judge whether the road will be safe for you to travel."

The two days passed by pleasantly enough, during which we rode round the station with Bracewell, to assist him in examining his sheep and to help in the various duties of a squatter's life.

Meantime, Toby and another native were sent out to ascertain what had become of the mob of blacks reported to be in the neighbourhood. They came back saying that, although they had come upon their tracks, the natives had moved away westward, and that we were not likely to fall in with them. We again, accordingly, told our host that we must go.

"Well, if you must, you must; and according to my promise I intend to ride part of the way with you," he answered. "I wish however that you could do without your baggage, and we would see how fast we could get over the ground; but as you have to take that, we must be content with a steady pace, and I'll make play on my way back so as to be at home again by night."

As there was a moon in the sky, and Bracewell knew every inch of the ground, we were in our saddles long before day-break, carrying with us our breakfast and kettle in which the tea could easily be made at the camp fire.

We had performed some ten or twelve miles before sunrise, enjoying the cool fresh air of early morning, and fresh it is even in Australia before the burning sun gains his power over the world.

We camped near a water-hole, from which we obtained all the fluid we required for our morning's meal. We had again mounted and were going round on the opposite side, when Bracewell exclaimed— "The blacks have been here. See, here are the remains of their fire still smouldering. They cannot have left it very long. We must keep a look-out for them when passing any spot from which they may hurl their lances should they be badly disposed; not that that is likely to be the case, and they certainly will not venture to attack us in the open."

Toby, who had examined the ground, gave it as his opinion that they had gone away to the northwards and that, being probably on a hunting expedition, they would be too intent on attacking their game to annoy us. Toby was right, and in about half an hour, just as we reached the top of a slight ridge or elevation which had before hidden them from view, we caught sight of several dusky figures, each holding in his hand a throwing-stick with a long spear attached to it. One of them had fixed to his left arm a shield of boughs which concealed his body as he crept towards a group of kangaroos feeding in the grassy bottom. As the hunters did not perceive us and we had time, we stood still watching them.

The throwing or throw-stick, is to serve the purpose of a sling for casting the spear. A heavy flat piece of wood, between two and three feet long, has at one end a slight hollow into which the end of the spear is fitted while at the other is a heavy weight, thus assisting the hunter in the act of throwing the spear. Except a small fillet of grass the natives wore not a particle of clothing, though there were several scarifications on their bodies; and what sailors call a sprit-sail-yard run through their nostrils which added to the ferocity of their appearance.

As we wanted to see how they would proceed, we kept as much as possible behind the ridge, and as the wind came from the kangaroos to us, we were not discovered by the animals. All this time the hunters were creeping forward, concealing themselves among the shrubs and trees until they got near enough to the game to hurl their spears with effect.

One fellow crept forward, holding his shield of boughs, until it seemed to us that he was almost close up to the kangaroos. Then his spear flew from his throwing-stick with so tremendous a force that the animal was almost pinned to the ground. Not a spear missed, and almost at the same moment

"EACH HOLDING IN HIS HAND A THROWING-STICK."

three kangaroos were killed. Three others hopped away, but were pursued by the nimble-footed hunters, who using their throwing-sticks as clubs, despatched the animals with reiterated blows on the head.

Not until the hunt was over did we show ourselves, when we astonished the savages standing over their slain game. Fixing their spears in their sticks they threatened to launch them against us should we attempt to deprive them of their prizes. On seeing this we directed Toby to say that we had no intention of interfering with them. Whether or not they understood him, however, we could not tell, for they stood without altering their position, and not wishing to have an encounter with them which must have ended in bloodshed, we made a wide circuit beyond the reach of their weapons. When we looked back we saw them joined by a large number of their fellows who were employed in dragging off the bodies of the kangaroos.

"I am afraid you will be in some danger from them on your return," I observed to Bracewell.

"No fear of that," he answered. "They will be too busy in gorging themselves with the flesh of the kangaroos; besides they will not be on the look-out for me, and a well-mounted man, provided he doesn't come unexpectedly on a mob, need have no fear of them. My rifle can carry farther than their throwing sticks, a fact of which they are well aware."

We soon lost sight of the blacks, and after riding on several miles further, our friend told us that he must bid us farewell, promising, however, to ride over to Mr. Strong's station, should he find he could leave home, to see how we were getting on. "And remember," he added, "I shall be glad if one or both of you can join me, should you not find yourselves comfortable at your relative's; and if he has moved on, as he intended doing, to another station, come back if you think fit at once; though probably, if he expects you, he will have left word that you may be forwarded on to him. He has, I understand, a large family, but as we have never met I cannot give you a description of them. I need not warn you to keep as good a watch at night as you have hitherto done, and to avoid either blacks or suspicious looking white men, though I do not mean to say that you are to look upon every traveller you meet with as a bush-ranger."

We having again thanked Bracewell for his advice and the hospitality he had shown us, he turned his horse's head towards his home, and we proceeded on our journey.

CHAPTER IV.

WE had already, according to our calculation, performed the distance to Mr. Strong's station, but no signs of it could we discover. The heat was oppressive, and seeing a wood on our left, we were assured from the nature of the trees, that either a water-hole or a stream would be found. We agreed to camp there for a couple of hours to let our horses feed and to take our dinner, hoping then by pushing on that we should before evening at all events arrive at the station. I had ridden forward to look out for the water, when just as I caught sight of the glitter of a pool, I saw two persons emerge from the shade. They were white lads with a couple of dogs and had guns in their hands. So intent were they on some object before them that they did not perceive me. One of them fired at an opossum which they had, I concluded, driven out of its hole. The animal fell to the ground, when they dashed forward to save it from being torn to pieces by the dogs. As they did so, one of them looked up and saw me watching them.

"Hallo! Where do you come from?" he exclaimed advancing.

"From England," I answered. "We want to

reach Mr. Strong's station, and shall be obliged if you will help us to find it."

"That's where we live, so we can take you to it," replied the lad. "You have, however, come somewhat out of your way, and must have passed it on your right."

I thanked him. "And who are you?" I asked.

"We are Mr. Strong's sons," he replied. "We came here to look for some stray cattle which are hid in this scrub, so we shall first have to drive them out, but that won't take us long. We left our horses hobbled close at hand while we stopped, intending to take our dinner, as we have been out since the morning."

"We were going to do the same," I obesrved. "Here comes my brother Guy; if you haven't eaten your dinner you'll join us, won't you?"

"Of course!" he said laughing. "And I conclude that you are Guy and Maurice Thurston, our cousins we have been expecting out from the old country for some months past. My name is Hector. That is my brother Oliver. I suppose you have heard of us?"

I had to confess that I had not before heard their names, though I did not like to say how little I knew about them.

Guy, Toby, and I, having dismounted and allowed our horses to drink at the pool, hobbled them and let them go away to feed, while we sat down in a shady spot to discuss our provisions. Our cousins produced damper, cold beef and cheese from their pockets; while Toby placed before us a piece of a kangaroo

"THEY WERE WHITE LADS WITH A COUPLE OF DOGS."

which we had shot the previous day and some biscuits, while we all contented ourselves with a draught of water from the pool.

The meal was quickly despatched, when our cousins jumped up saying that they must look out for the cattle, and that as soon as we saw the herd rounded up and clear of the scrub, we might follow in the rear. They advised us to take care should any of them charge us, as they were apt to be vicious, and Toby might have a difficulty in escaping. "You need not hurry yourselves," they added, "but when you hear the sound of our stock whips, you had better mount and be ready to start."

Guy and I agreed that it was very fortunate we had fallen in with our cousins, who seemed to be wonderfully hardy fellows, and we hoped might prove good companions.

We waited a short time, when we heard, coming from some distance, apparently, the sharp report of the whips, like the sound of crackers. Now the sounds, mingled with a chorus of lowing and bellowing, reached us from one side, now from the other, every moment approaching nearer, so that we agreed that it would be wise to catch our horses and mount. We were quickly in our saddles, when several bulls burst out of the scrub a short distance from us. We rode forward to get out of their way as they looked very much inclined to charge us. Presently others appeared in different directions, and then our two young cousins, cracking their long whips, followed, rounding up the cattle in the most scientific manner, and turning several cows which with their calves were evidently intent on bolting back into the scrub.

We soon got excited with the scene, and although our horses were somewhat tired and we had no stock whips, we managed so effectually to turn the cattle with our ordinary riding whips, that our cousins declared we assisted them very much. The mob once collected went on steadily until we got them into the paddock, an enclosure half a mile in extent, into which, some bars being removed, most of them eagerly rushed. A few however tried to bolt, but were sent back by the stock whips, and all were fortunately turned in; some to be used for beef, others for branding, while the cows were wanted for milking.

"Where is the station?" I asked. "I can see only this immense paddock."

"There!" answered Hector, pointing to where I caught sight of the roofs of several low buildings. "We shall soon be there."

We put our horses into a canter, and in a short time arrived before a collection of buildings like Indian bungalows, the centre of which was the dwelling house, which had slab walls and shingled roof, with a pretty verandah in front.

A stout gentleman, a few grey hairs sprinkling his head and large bushy beard, came out to meet us, and on hearing from Hector who we were, welcomed us cordially.

Our cousins took our horses, which they turned into a small paddock containing a shed at one end to afford shelter to the animals.

We then entered the house, where we were introduced to the hostess, a tall lady, somewhat sallow and careworn, but with considerable animation in her manner. We were next made known to three young ladies, two of whom we understood were Misses Strong and a third Clara Mayne, a friend; besides these there were three young children. In a short time, two tall lads, sunburnt, and sinewy, made their appearance with stock whips in their hands and broad-brimmed hats on their heads.

"You have not seen them all yet," observed our hostess.

Two more young men came in, one somewhat older than Guy, the other about my own age, and I found that they also were cousins. Altogether a goodly company sat down to the evening meal. We all waited on ourselves, there being no female helps in the household.

A rattling conversation was kept up, the young men describing to their father the events of the day, while we had to give an account of our adventures from the time of our landing. They were all highly interested in hearing of Bracewell being stuck up by bushrangers and how we had rescued him.

"We must put a stop to the career of those gentlemen," observed Mr. Strong. "We have heard before this of their doings, and I have even considered it prudent not to leave the ladies alone in the house without two or three men as guards; a most abominable inconvenience, and yet, from knowing the atrocities of which they are capable, I consider it absolutely necessary."

The blacks, he said, had also been troublesome. A

large mob who had been wandering about in that part of the country, might, he thought it possible, take it into their heads, to pay the station a visit; though it was not likely that they would do harm should they find his people prepared for them.

After a pleasant evening, we were shown to the room we were to occupy in one of the other sheds where three of our cousins also slept. One of the elder ones was called in the night to mount guard, and we found that a watch was regularly kept in case either bushrangers or blacks should make their appearance.

Next morning our cousins invited us to accompany them to drive in another mob of cattle for the purpose of mustering and branding the calves. We proposed riding our own horses, but they laughed at the notion.

"You'd get run down to a certainty," said Hector. "As we go along I'll tell you what you'll have to do, for there's nothing like beginning at once."

We were in the saddle before daylight, having first breakfasted, when we found a mob of sixty or eighty tame cattle, a short distance from the station.

"What are they for?" I asked.

"They are coaches!" answered Hector. "We use them to entice the wild ones, who take shelter among them, and then the whole are more easily driven into the stock yards."

The animals quietly pursued their way, going wherever their drivers chose to direct them. We mustered a dozen horsemen. On arriving close to the run where the wild cattle were known to be, three of the men remained with the coaches, and the rest of us rode

"CRACKING OUR WHIPS AND SHOUTING." [p. 77.

forward, dividing into two parties, the one going to the right, the other to the left, so as to encircle the whole camp,—the name given to the spot where the wild cattle congregate. The country had a very wild appearance, there were rocks and hills and fallen trees in all directions, and I guessed that we should have a pretty rough ride. Our object was to drive the cattle towards the coaches and to prevent any of them turning back and breaking through the line we formed in their rear. We were accompanied, I should have said, by a pack of dogs, of a somewhat mongrel appearance, of all sizes and shapes. On arriving at the camp one of the best mounted stockmen went ahead to lead the cattle, which curiously enough always follow where they see another animal going, and now the work began.

Cracking our whips and shouting at the top of our voices, off we started over the rough ground, now dashing up a hill, now descending the steep side of another, our animals springing and dodging about to avoid rocks and other obstructions. Now we leaped over trees, twisting and turning in every direction to avoid the standing stumps and jumping over scattered logs; now we had to force our way through a thick patch of saplings which caught us as in a net. Not occasionally but every moment some of the cattle would turn and attempt to break through, some of our party having immediately to wheel round, with loud cracks of their whips, and make the beasts head the other way. None of us seemed to think of the danger we were running. Though Guy and I were good horsemen it was pretty hard work for us, and our whips were but of little use as we could not make them crack like the rest of the party. The cows gave us most trouble, but the dogs hung on to the animals, some catching them by the nose, others by the heels or tails, not ceasing to worry them until they took the required direction.

As we were riding along, after we had got free of the bush, a huge bull made a dash out, attempting to escape. I galloped after him, belabouring him with my whip, and in spite of his continuing to try and toss me, turned him back into the herd.

"Well done, Maurice," exclaimed Hector, "you'll make a first-rate stockman, but you must practise with your whip before you can become as expert as is necessary."

We visited, in the course of a day or two, other camps in which the wild cattle were collected in the same fashion; when, led by the coaches, the whole were driven into the yards, as they are called, situated at the head station. Here they were allowed to remain until next morning when the operation of mustering and branding commenced. The yard was so divided that the cattle required for the various purposes were driven into different compartments; the calves into one, the cattle to be slaughtered into another, and those to be turned loose again, into a third, while the stockmen from two or three neighbouring stations attended to claim any of their masters' cattle which had got in among Mr. Strong's.

A calf having been lassoed, it was hauled up and its head held down by a plank, when a hot brand was handed to a man standing ready to press it against the creature's skin, where an indelible mark was left, when the little bellower was allowed to rise and make its escape into another pen.

Guy and I were not of much use, but we saw everything going forward, and lent a hand whenever we could.

"Now, my lads," said Mr. Strong to us the next day; " I see the stuff you are made of. You'll do, and if you like to remain with me to learn all you ought to know, you are welcome; after that you can decide what course you will follow."

We had been some days at the station when a person arrived who had occasionally been spoken of as Mr. Kimber. He acted as tutor to our host's younger sons as he did also to another family in the neighbourhood. He was a graduate of one of our leading universities, and had been found by Mr. Strong in the humble capacity of hut-keeper on a neighbouring station, a situation he was compelled to take in consequence of having expended the whole of his means. His present occupation was more in accordance with his tastes, although his salary was, I suspect, not very considerable. He was evidently not cut out for an Australian settler, for though he could manage to stick on horseback, as Hector observed, " he preferred a walk to a gallop;" while he persisted in wearing a stovepipe hat and a swallow-tail coat, which he evidently considered a more dignified costume than the straw hat and red shirt generally worn by all ranks in the bush. He was amusing from the simplicity of his remarks, and as he was honest and well-informed, Mr. Strong was really glad to retain him.

We had been expecting a visit from Bracewell, as

Guy had written to him to tell him that we were still remaining with our relative, who did not appear to have any idea of leaving his station, but he had received no answer.

Mr. Kimber gave two days of the week to the family of a Captain Mason, who owned the station next to Mr. Strong's. His plan was to ride over early in the morning of one day and to return late in the evening of the next.

After we had become tolerably intimate he invited me to accompany him, and to assist in teaching two of the younger boys. As I wished to become acquainted with Captain Mason, and to see his station, I readily accepted his invitation. I found a family very similar to that of Mr. Strong, and quite as numerous; the girls and boys tall and lithe, but as active as crickets. The girls told me to tell my cousins that they would ride over some day to see them, as soon as those abominable bushrangers had been captured.

We started somewhat later than usual from Captain Mason's, but the "Dominie," as the boys called him, had frequently traversed the road, and assured me that he knew it perfectly. We pushed on, however, as fast as we could go, wishing to get in before dark, as my companion confided to me the fact that he felt not a little nervous about the bushrangers, of whose atrocious deeds the young Masons had been telling him—the murders they had committed, the huts they had attacked, and the number of people they had stuck up. I could not disprove the statements, though I believe the accounts greatly exaggerated,

"I CAUGHT SIGHT OF TWO HORSEMEN." [*p.* 84.

and I described to him the way we had driven the fellows off by the exhibition of firmness and courage.

"All very well in daylight," he observed; "but suppose the villains were to pop up from behind the bushes on the other side of the road, and order us to stand and deliver, and to threaten to shoot us if we attempted to draw our pistols,—and by the bye I haven't any to draw,—what should we do?"

"Put spurs to our horses and gallop out of their way," I answered. "They wouldn't dare to fire, and if they did, the chances are they would miss us. We must run some danger in this country, and the risk is not nearly so great as riding after wild cattle as we have still to do, so pray do not make yourself unhappy on the subject."

Still, I saw that my companion looked anxiously about him, especially as it began to grow dusk, immediately after which darkness came on, and we were compelled to moderate our speed for fear of getting a knock on our heads from overhanging branches, or riding against fallen logs.

Eager as the dominie was to get on, not being a first-rate horseman he went even slower than was necessary. We were passing through a thickish part of the forest, when, reining in his steed, he whispered to me in a tremulous voice—"Pull up, pray do, I hear the tramp of horses' feet. Suppose they should be bushrangers, they might shoot us down before we had time to escape."

I reined in my steed to listen for the sounds which his sensitive ear had detected. "They may be simply wild cattle, or riderless horses, taking a scamper," I observed, laughing.

"Oh, no; they don't move about after dark," he said; "they must be mounted horses, do let us remain quiet until we ascertain who the people are"

"They are very likely some of the young Strongs coming out to meet us," I remarked.

Scarcely had I said this, however, than I caught sight of two horsemen riding across an open glade some distance off. There was sufficient light for me to make out the figures distinctly. One was a big fellow in a rough garb, the other was slighter, and both were armed. Presently afterwards two others came into view, the moonbeams glancing on the barrels of their rifles, showing that they also were armed. I fully expected that they would discover us, and I intended if they did so boldly to ride up and enquire where they were going. They galloped on, however, without perceiving us. As I alone had arms I felt that it would be folly to interfere with them, as we might run the risk of being shot, while we could gain no possible advantage. I therefore remained perfectly quiet, and in another minute they were out of sight. They were going in the direction of Captain Mason's station. They would be, however, mistaken, I hoped, if they expected to surprise our friends; who had assured me that they kept a watch by night and day, and were well prepared for such gentry.

As soon as they were out of hearing, we rode on; the dominie I saw feeling far from happy, as every now and then he turned his head over his shoulder to assure himself that we were not followed.

The moon, which had now risen high in the sky, afforded us ample light to see our way. As the country became more open, we were able to push on as fast as we could go.

We were to have another adventure. While still some distance from home, the loud lowing of a cow reached our ears. The animal was evidently alarmed at something. Galloping towards it, we found on getting up that she was endeavouring to protect her calf from the attack of a dozen dingoes. Now she would run at one with her sharp horns, now at another, but the moment she had gone in one direction the brutes would assail her helpless young one. They were not even deterred by our approach.

"We must put an end to these dingoes!" I exclaimed. Unstrapping one of my stirrup irons and using it as a weapon, I singled out one of the wild dogs, and succeeded, after several attempts, in giving it a blow on the head which brought it to the ground. I then attacked another, which I treated in the same fashion. The dominie tried to imitate me but very nearly tumbled over on his nose, though he assisted in protecting the calf by driving off the cowardly brutes. The cow at last pinned one to the ground with her horns, and then turning round attacked it with her heels until she well-nigh pounded it into a jelly. At length the survivors took to flight.

"We have killed three at at all events," remarked the dominie.

"Not so sure of that," I answered as we rode away, and turning my head, I observed that one of the dingoes was beginning to move. I turned round, when it lay perfectly still, but it had crept on half a dozen yards at least.

I gave it a few more blows with my stirrup iron, and then getting out my knife cut its throat. I treated its companions in the same manner, as I did not feel sure that the one the cow had tossed was really dead, so tenacious of life are the brutes.

I do not know whether the cow was grateful, but we left her licking her calf where the dingoes had bitten it. When we drew in sight of the station we saw Hector and his elder brother Ralph coming to meet us.

"We got somewhat anxious about your being so much later than usual," said the latter. "We have had a visit from some suspicious characters who said that they were in search of work and had lost their way, and begged that they might have a night's lodging in one of the out-houses, and some supper and breakfast, and that one or two of us would ride along with them in the morning to show them the road to the next station. As, however, Hector had detected a brace of pistols under the shirt of the man who spoke, and saw that the others had long knives in their belts, while their countenances were of the most villainous cast, we refused to comply with their wishes, and told them that they must ride on and camp out as they had evidently previously been doing."

"I did not think all had villainous countenances," said Hector; "there was one good-looking young fellow among them. He kept in the background and said nothing. However, I had no doubt of what they were, and they showed it by riding away when they found that we were not to be taken in. Oliver followed them, when they stopped at a piece of scrub, from which they each drew forth a rifle and several other articles, still further proving that they had some treacherous design in coming to the station."

CHAPTER V.

THE account we brought of the direction the supposed bushrangers were riding convinced Mr. Strong that such was their character, and that pressed for food and ammunition, probably for both, they were going to some other station to supply their wants by force. We, however, heard nothing of them, nor had they, we found, visited Captain Mason's station, and in what direction they had gone we could not ascertain.

Some days after the events I have described, a stockman who had been engaged by Mr. Strong's agent arrived. He had stopped at Bracewell's, and brought the sad intelligence that our friend was ill, and that he had expressed a strong wish that either Guy or I should come and stay with him. He also greatly wanted medical advice. No doctor was to be found within sixty miles of the station. Guy and I were eager to go to the assistance of our friend, and Mr. Strong gave both of us leave. Hector having some business to transact for his father at the chief town, and the dominie, who we found had a considerable amount of medical knowledge, offered to go if he could be spared for a few days. To this Mr. Strong did not object, and before daylight the next morning

"THREE KANGAROOS LEISURELY CROPPING THE GRASS." [*p.* 91.

we set off carrying huge saddle-bags in which the articles we required were stowed. Those of the dominie contained his medicine chest—not a very large one, but well suited for the bush, where Morrison's pills are more in request than drugs in general. We were accompanied by two dogs, one of which had from my first arrival especially attached himself to me, and Hector, to whom he belonged, had made me a present of him.

Though anxious about our friend we were all in high spirits at the prospect of a gallop across the country, which few people in good health could fail to enjoy. Even the dominie forgot his fears of bush-rangers and mials, or wild blacks.

Our road lay through a lightly timbered country, and here and there patches of scrub consisting of a sweet-scented wattle. We saw pigeons in abundance, and at times a kangaroo hopped away before us. The grass, owing to the heat of the weather, was rather yellow than green, but we knew that a few showers would soon change its hue. After traversing this country for several miles, we saw some trees evidently much larger than those round us. As we drew near, the vegetation below us looked green, a sign that we were approaching a creek or water-hole. Just then we caught sight of three kangaroos leisurely cropping the grass. Before, however, we could unsling our rifles, they winded us and bounded away at a rate which would have made it hopeless to follow them unless we had been accompanied by native dogs and were prepared for a long chase. We accordingly unsaddled at the hole, which was full of unusually clear water, a luxury not often obtained in the bush. The grass, also, beneath the trees being shaded was closer and greener than that elsewhere; they were mostly tea-trees and gum-trees, many of them growing to a good size. Among the boughs we saw numbers of white cockatoos, parrots, laughing jackasses, and many other birds, who received us, as we prepared to camp for our noonday meal, with a loud chorus of varied cries.

Having allowed our horses some time to feed, we again mounted and rode forward. We camped again at night at another water-hole, and were at an early hour the next morning once more in our saddles.

We had proceeded some little distance, when I observed that Guy's horse had gone lame, and presently it made a fearful stumble from which he could with difficulty recover it.

"I am afraid that I must get off and walk, and give the horse a chance of recovering himself," said Guy.

We pulled up, and Hector examined the animal's hoofs. A sharp thorn had run into his right fore-foot, and though Hector extracted it, the animal still remained as lame as before. We should not, under ordinary circumstances, have minded the delay, but knowing how ill Bracewell was we were much annoyed.

At last Hector offered to remain with Guy, if the dominie and I would ride on. To this proposal I was very glad to accede.

The dominie at first looked a little uncomfortable at having to proceed with a single companion.

" Suppose we were to fall in with bushrangers," he observed. " What should we do ? "

" Shoot them through the head if they offer to interfere with you," said Hector. " You are always thinking of those fellows. The chances are they cleared out of our district long ago when they found that we were prepared for them."

" You may do our friend Bracewell a great deal of good," I observed, " for you at all events know more about doctoring than any of us. You can discover what is the matter with him."

" I certainly will not decline doing what you say," he answered, and seeing to our saddle-girths we prepared for a gallop which would bring us up to Bracewell's station before nightfall, Hector and Guy promising to follow as fast as they could, although they would have to camp out another night. We started off. The dominie had lately improved in his horsemanship, and we made good play over the ground. I felt sure that I knew the way, as the track between the two stations was tolerably well defined. There were only two places, of no great extent, passing through which we should have to pull rein. At the first the ground was unusually rough and rocky, with thick underwood. We got over it, however, and soon afterwards had to pass through a gorge in the only range of hills we had to cross. The path was narrow, so that we could not conveniently ride side by side. I therefore, as guide, took the lead, and had unintentionally got some way ahead of the dominie, when I heard him cry out, and turning round to see what was the matter I found my right arm seized by a fellow who had sprung out from behind a rock while another grasped my horse's rein, and the next instant I was dragged to the ground.

"Stuck up at last, young master," cried a voice which I recognised as that of the tall bushranger Guy and I had before encountered and driven off. "Do not be a fool and show fight, or I'll blow your brains out. Here, hand out what you've got about you. You may think yourself fortunate if we leave you the clothes on your back, but we don't want them. Do as I tell you, down on your knees and stay there, while I feel your pockets."

As may be supposed I did not carry much money in the bush, but on leaving home I had put a couple of sovereigns in my pocket. My rifle, of course, I expected to lose.

While the bushranger was performing the operation of cleaning me out, a savage bull-dog approached, and I thought was going to fly at me, but I found his eyes were directed towards some object at my back, which proved to be my faithful Carlo, who, however ready to do battle in my cause, thought it prudent, in the presence of a superior force, to yield to circumstances.

All this time I could not see what was happening to the dominie, but I concluded that he would wisely not attempt to make any resistance, and that he was being cleaned out as I was. I did not again hear his voice, and as the bushranger swore that he would shoot me through the head should I move, I thought it as well not to look round lest he should put his threat into execution. The fellow who had taken my

STUCK UP BY BUSHRANGERS. [p. 94.

horse now picked up my gun and carried it off to a short distance. Two of them then produced a rope, intending, I concluded, to treat the dominie and me as they had Bracewell.

As the man who stood over me returned his pistol to his belt, I took a glance round to try and ascertain what had become of my companion, but he was nowhere to be seen, and I feared, therefore, that they intended to bind him to a tree at such a distance that we could hold no communication with each other. My dog Carlo was also not to be seen; I felt, however, nearly sure that the bushrangers had not carried him off. I had often remarked his peculiar sagacity, and hoped that, finding he could do me no good, he had kept out of the way to avoid the risk of being either killed or captured. I soon found that my anticipations were correct. The bushranger now holding a pistol to my head made me get up and walk to a tree some distance from the track, so that should any travellers pass by I should not be discovered. I might have acted a more heroic part had I struggled desperately, seized a pistol, and attempted to blow out the brains of one of the ruffians; but as I felt that it was more than likely I should lose my own life, I considered it wiser to yield with calmness and dignity.

The villains were well up to their work, and having secured my hands behind me, they fastened me in so effectual a way to a tree, that I could not possibly set myself at liberty.

Without speaking another word to me, the big bushranger led off my horse, carrying with him my gun and articles he had taken from me, and disappeared among the trees. I saw two other persons leading a horse, going in the same direction, one of whom I felt sure, from his figure, was Vinson, though I did not see his countenance. Indeed, I suspect that he had unintentionally avoided coming near me.

As soon as the bushrangers had gone, I looked round in search of the dominie, but could nowhere discover him. I could scarcely hope that he had escaped, or, if he had, that he had got off on horseback. I felt nearly sure that the horse I had just seen led away by the robbers was his. I was thus left in doubt how they had treated him, whether they had bound him as they had me, or used greater violence. As soon as I fancied that they had gone off to a sufficient distance not to hear me, I shouted to the dominie, hoping to hear a reply. Not a sound reached my ears, and I began seriously to apprehend that they had knocked him on the head or stabbed him. I remembered the dread he had always expressed of the bushrangers, and I thought it possible that he might have had some especial reason for fearing them. Perhaps he had known one of them, or might have attempted at some time or other to betray them into the hands of the police.

After shouting in vain for some minutes, I began to lose all hope of receiving a reply. What had become of Carlo, I could not tell; I feared that the bushrangers must have killed him, as I felt nearly sure that he would not have deserted me, either to make his escape from the scene of danger, or to follow them. I should have been glad to have him by my side for the sake of companionship; it also struck me that should he come, he might possibly be able to bite through the thongs if I could show him what I wanted done. I called to him several times, but he did not appear. At last I arrived at the conclusion that the bushrangers had killed him. I now began to think of my own dangerous position, while thus utterly unable to defend myself. If discovered by hostile blacks, they would make me a target for their spears, or a pack of dingoes might attack me. I never had heard of their assaulting a living man, but I saw no reason why they should not do so, should they discover that I had no means of defending myself. A snake or scorpion might bite me, and mosquitoes or other stinging insects were sure to find me out and annoy me; while I had the prospect of remaining without water or food for hours, or perhaps days to come, when I might at last perish from hunger and thirst. Such and other gloomy thoughts passed through my mind. I had not from the first struggled, for I felt sure that I should thus tighten the thongs which bound me. Now, however, I set to work calmy to try and release myself, by drawing up one of my hands, hoping that if I could but get my head low enough to reach the thong round my arm, I might in time gnaw it through; but after making a variety of efforts I found that the attempt was vain, and giving it up, I resigned myself to my fate, whatever that might be.

Still it must be understood that I did not altogether lose hope. There was the possible chance of the dominie having escaped, and that some traveller might be coming by and release me, as Guy and I had released Bracewell. Still many hours might pass before then, and I was already suffering from thirst, though I was not troubled by hunger. Being out of the path, I could only hope to attract attention from passers-by by shouting as I heard the sound of their horses' footsteps. This I could do as long as I retained my senses, but I might, I feared, drop off into a state of stupor, and those who might have released me might be close at hand without my knowing it.

Suddenly I thought I would make one more attempt to ascertain if the dominie was within hearing. I shouted as loud as I could bawl, and then gave a cooey, which would reach further than any other sound. I listened; a faint cry came from a distance. It was the dominie's voice, I thought, but could not make out what he said. The tones were melancholy in the extreme. It might be some consolation to him, poor fellow, to know that I was alive, and I no longer doubted that the bushrangers had treated him in the same manner that they had me, though I suspected that he had been either stunned or so frightened that he had not before heard my shouts or been able to reply. I intended every now and then to give him a hail, when it occurred to me that our voices might attract any blacks passing at a distance, and that we should thus increase the risk of being killed by them.

I could scarcely tell how the hours went by. At length darkness came on, and I began to doze. It was the best thing I could do, as it prevented me from feeling either hunger or thirst. I was, however, quickly awakened by the thongs cutting my limbs as I bent forward. I then tried to lean against the tree with my feet out, and in that position I escaped the pressure on my limbs, and was at last able to drop off to sleep. My slumbers, as may be supposed, were far from pleasant, indeed I was conscious all the time that something disagreeable had happened; but still, by thus snatching a few intervals of sleep, I found that the night passed away faster than I should have supposed possible. Strange sounds occasionally reached my ears. I fancied that I heard in the distance the yelping and barking of a pack of dingoes, and as the brutes often hunt together in considerable numbers, I dreaded that they might find out the dominie and me, and tear us to pieces. With intense relief I saw the streaks of dawn appear in the sky. The laughing jackass uttered his cheerful notes, and parrots and other birds began to chirp and screech and chatter. The sound tended somewhat to raise my spirits, though the pangs of hunger and thirst which now oppressed me soon became insupportable. As in daylight the blacks might be passing, I was afraid of attracting their attention by crying out, so that I was unable to ascertain how it fared with the poor dominie. When the sun rose, the heat became oppressive, and the insects began to buzz about my face, while I had no power to drive them off.

This annoyance was trying in the extreme. I spluttered and spat, and winked my eyes, and shook my head, to very little effect; and although the creatures did not often bite me, their buzzing and

"HE MIGHT HAVE BEEN MISTAKEN FOR A BRONZE STATUE."
[p. 104.

tickling almost drove me mad. At last a sound struck my ear. It was the bay of a hound, then came a bark, and the next instant the faithful Carlo bounded up to me, and licking my face, soon drove off the flies. Then, having exhibited his delight, away he went barking cheerfully. Presently the sound of the tramping of horses' hoofs reached my ears, but on a sudden, the sound ceased, and I feared that I had been deceived; but then it occurred to me that the rider had discovered the dominie, and was stopping to set him at liberty. In a few seconds I caught sight of a horseman. It was my brother Guy, who came galloping up to me. Throwing himself from his saddle, without stopping to ask questions he cut the thongs which bound me to the tree.

"You looked so pale that I thought that was the first thing to do," said Guy, as he supported me in his arms, and gradually let me sink down on the ground, for I could not stand. "Hector is looking after the dominie, he is even in a worse condition than you are."

"I am fearfully thirsty," I said.

"I knew you must be," he replied, applying a water-bottle to my mouth.

The draught, which was tolerably cool, had an almost instantaneous effect, and I was at once able to get up on my feet.

"We thought something had happened when Carlo, rushing back, came barking and pulling at our trousers; and as soon as we could catch our horses, in spite of the lameness of mine, we started off. We could not travel fast at night, but immediately day broke we galloped on; and I am thankful indeed, my dear Maurice, to find you uninjured—but how did you get into this plight?"

I briefly told him of the way the bushrangers had stuck me up.

"The villains! I wish that we could find them. Now, get up on my horse, and we will go to where I left Hector and the dominie. We'll breakfast as soon as we can reach a water-hole. We passed one a little way back, and we must then try and get on to Bracewell's as soon as possible."

With his assistance, I mounted his horse, and we soon reached the spot where Hector was attending to the dominie, who was slowly recovering. I really believe, from the condition he was in, that he would soon have died. One of the ruffians had struck him over the head with the butt of his pistol, but he had suffered more from fear than from the blow, for he fully believed that they were going to put him to death. He was lifted on Hector's horse, and we soon reached the water-hole. The fire was quickly lighted, and after a good breakfast on a paddy-melon —a small species of kangaroo—which Hector had shot the previous evening, we felt greatly revived, and fully able to continue the journey; indeed, I felt myself as strong as ever. Guy and Hector ran alongside the horses, and we made good progress. We had reached an open part of the country, when we caught sight of a figure seated on a fallen log. His back was towards us, and he did not appear to notice our approach; indeed, so motionless did he sit, that he might have been mistaken for a bronze statue. He had not a rag round his body, but on his shoulders were a number of raised marks, produced by making slashes in the skin, and filling them up with clay, so that when the wound healed, an elevated scar was made. His hair was fastened in a top-knot, and he had a long pointed beard, with moustache on his lips, his prominent nose having nothing of the negro character about it. Fastened to a belt round his waist was a snake and a little kangaroo rat, on which he evidently intended to make his dinner. A cord round his neck supported a shell ornament in front, and a tassel behind completed his costume. I describe him, of course, not as we saw him when at a distance, but according to the appearance he presented on a further acquaintance. Suddenly, as we came upon him, he seemed in no way alarmed; but, jumping up, he seized his spear and throwing-stick which lay on the ground at his side. Seeing, however, that he could not possibly escape us, he made no attempt to run.

As we approached, Hector, who from a long intercourse with the blacks was able to make him understand what he said, inquired whether he had seen any white men passing that way, and should he have done so, whether he could tell us who they were.

The black, without hesitation, replied, saying, that he had seen no less than four, that they were armed with guns, and were leading a couple of horses.

"That looks suspicious. They must have been the bushrangers," observed Hector; "and if—as I think possible—they are not far off, we must try and capture the fellows, or at all events recover our horses."

Hector, who closely questioned the black, was satisfied that he wished to be honest, and accordingly asked him if he thought that he could track the bushrangers. He replied, without hesitation, that if he once came upon their trail he could do so.

"Lead on, then," said Hector.

Anxious as we were to get to Bracewell's, it was important to recover our horses, and if possible to capture the robbers. We were five against four, for having promised the black a handsome reward, if we should catch one or more of the villains, we could trust to his aid, and his spear would be of as much use as our guns at close quarters; but we could not reckon much on the assistance of the dominie, whose nervousness we thought would prevent him from doing what was necessary.

We had not gone far, when the black declared positively, that he had found the trail of the robbers, and that probably they would be encamped at a waterhole not far off.

Our undertaking was one requiring the greatest caution, for they were certain to be on the watch, and being well armed, would prove formidable opponents. We might, to be sure, steal upon them during the darkness of night and shoot them down, but we had no wish to do that; our object was to recover our property and bring them to justice. The black showed himself to be an admirable scout. The evening was drawing on when he told us that we were not far from where he expected to find them.

How it happened that they had not ridden to a distance, it was impossible to say; probably the spot they had chosen, being out of the high road, they did not expect to be discovered.

Securing our horses in a thick scrub, where they were completely concealed, we cautiously advanced, the black going ahead. It was by this time getting quite dark. Our great fear was that the dog they had with them would wind us, and if so it would be necessary to shoot the creature as it approached. This, of course, would give them the alarm, though we hoped to spring upon them and knock over two or three before they could escape. The horses were probably feeding at a distance, and the saddles and baggage would be at the camp.

We were noiselessly making our way, when the black signed to us to halt, and then began to creep forward. Anxious to have a look at the fellows I followed his example, carrying my pistols in my belt, and I found that Carlo was close at my heels, evidently aware that danger was at hand. At last the black stopped, when I joined him; and looking over some low shrubs, I saw the four bushrangers seated round a fire, their saddles and baggage and their guns lying on the ground near them. They evidently did not suppose that there was any chance of their being attacked. The only one of their party who seemed to be on the watch was their bull-dog, who, lifting up his head, turned his eyes towards us. The wind was blowing from them to us, or the dog would have smelt us out. As it was I fully expected every moment to see him dash forward with a loud bark to where we lay. I did not dare to move, and scarcely, indeed, to breathe.

After watching for some time, the black began slowly to retreat, and I was truly thankful when we got out of hearing of their voices.

CHAPTER VI.

WHEN I got back to my friends we held a consultation as to our best mode of proceeding. It was agreed that we would wait until the bushrangers separated, which they were sure to do in the morning, and then rush on those in the camp while the others were away. The dog would prove the chief obstacle, and it was settled that I was to shoot him while Hector and Guy should dash into their camp. Two of the men would in all probability remain, while the others went to look after the horses, leaving their arms behind them. The dominie was to remain with the horses in case any of the fellows escaping might gallop off with them.

We waited until about a couple of hours to dawn, when we crept forward, led by the black. We dared not approach as close as we could have wished, on account of their watch-dog, who would be certain to give the alarm. Our plans being arranged, the dominie and I lay down, and, wearied with what we had lately gone through, slept for the greater part of the night.

It was still dusk when, having crept up to the robbers' camp, we saw one of them get up and throw some sticks on the fire. He then aroused his companions, and two of them, the big bushranger and one

I took to be Vinson, went off, as we concluded, to bring in the horses, happily leaving their guns behind them.

Now was our opportunity. At a signal from Hector, we rose to our feet, and holding our guns ready to fire, rushed towards the two men, who were engaged in cooking their breakfast. The bull-dog, with a fierce bark, sprang towards us. As he did so, the black with his spear nearly fixed the brute to the ground, which saved me from having to fire, and thus alarming the other two. One of the men attempted to take up his gun, but it was beyond his reach; he, however, seized from the fire a thick stick, with which he made a blow at my head; but at that instant my brave Carlo sprang at his throat with a force which brought him to the ground. Hector and Guy were in the meantime struggling with the other man, whom they succeeded in securing. Having lashed his arms behind him, they were at liberty to come to my assistance, and soon firmly bound the fellow Carlo had overthrown, for I had not struck a blow. On examining the countenances of the men we discovered that they were both strangers. The big bushranger and Vinson, who were, we had little doubt, the other two we had seen, had gone off probably to catch the horses. Having left their arms behind them they were in our power, but it was a great question whether we could manage to capture them. They would probably be back in a few minutes, and we had at once to decide how to act.

"I have a bright idea," exclaimed Guy; "I tell you what we will do. We'll gag these two fellows to prevent them from crying out, and drag them behind those bushes close to the camp. You, Maurice, and the black, being also concealed, must threaten to shoot them if they attempt to make any noise. Hector and I will then take their places at the fire, and pretend to be cooking the breakfast. As there will not be much light for some time, the other men when they return will not at first discover us, and we shall be able to point our rifles and order them to give in before they are aware of the trap we have laid. To make things more certain, we'll put on our prisoners' cabbage straw hats and red shirts, so that the chances are that they will get close up before they find out their mistake."

Hector and I highly approving of Guy's suggestion, we immediately set about putting it into execution. The black, who, being a remarkably intelligent fellow, fully understood our object, seemed highly delighted, grinning from ear to ear, as he assisted us.

We quickly gagged our prisoners, and then, dragging them behind the bushes, took off their shirts and hats, which, as they were far from clean, I was secretly glad I had not got to wear. Guy and Hector put them on, and then examining the fire-arms to ascertain if they were properly loaded, drew them close to the fire, before which they sat down. While one turned the spits on which they had put some meat to roast, the other employed himself in chopping up sticks and placing them on the fire. So exactly did they act the parts in which we had found our present prisoners engaged, that I felt sure the other men would not suspect the trap laid for them until they were close up to the camp. It was to be hoped that both would come at the same time, for if not, though we might seize one, the other would probably be warned, and make his escape. There was a risk, of course, that they would come across the dominie and the horses, and if so, would guess that we had discovered their camp, and would at all events be on their guard. Guy had, however, especially charged the dominie that should the bushrangers by any accident discover him, he was to keep them at a distance by threatening to fire if they approached.

While my brother and Hector were bending over the fire as I have described, I kept peering through the bushes, keeping one eye on our two prisoners, though I felt sure that the black would watch them carefully as he squatted down by their side with a sharp knife in his hand. It was a nervous time, but we had not long to wait before we heard the dull sound of galloping feet, and several horses came in sight, followed by the big bushranger mounted on a powerful steed. I could nowhere see Vinson, so that he at all events would have a chance of escaping. The horses came rushing on, and as they got near the fire separated, some on one side, some on the other. With an oath the big man shouted out—

"Why don't you stop them, you fellows?" The two figures bending over the fire did not appear to hear him, until, throwing himself from his horse, he approached them; when, snatching up their rifles, they suddenly turned round and presented the barrels at his head.

"Hands up, or we fire!" cried Guy and Hector in the same breath.

"BRAVE CARLO SPRANG UPON HIM." [*p.* 119.

Notwithstanding this warning the bushranger's right hand instantly moved towards the butt of the pistol in his belt, his left still holding the rein; he, however, quickly changed his mind, for he well knew, should he attempt to draw his weapon, before he could present it a couple of balls might be crashing through his brain. Another oath escaped his lips.

"Caught at last," he cried out, as if he was going to yield, but the next instant with a bound he was in his saddle, leaning forward at the same time, so that the horse's neck might protect his head. Guy fired.

The bullet only grazed the fellow's shoulder. I was taking aim at the fugitive, when another person appeared, driving before him the remainder of the horses. Forgetting for a moment that the bushranger's guns lay beside my brother and Hector, but recollecting that the big fellow had a brace of pistols in his belt, I was afraid of firing lest I should miss; and that he, coming back, would turn the tables on us. The next instant Hector and Guy had each picked up a gun. The big bushranger had, however, already got to a considerable distance, and although both fired, he continued his course, apparently uninjured.

While they were reloading, the fourth man, whom I took to be Vinson, had disappeared. We all three immediately rushed out to stop the horses, and succeeded in catching our own and two others. Our own saddles were in the robber's camp, so all we had to do was to put them on ready for a start. We then placed our prisoners on the backs of the other two, securing their legs under the horses' bellies, and fastening long leathern thongs to the bridles. We then, carrying off the ammunition, and two of the guns as trophies, smashed up the others, and threw the saddles and the few articles of baggage we found, on the fire, retaining, however, one or two things which were likely to prove acceptable to our black guide, who was highly delighted with his share of the plunder. Hoping to receive a further reward, he undertook to accompany us to Bracewell's, and to lead our prisoners' horses. We thought it prudent, however, not to trust him too much, though we accepted his offer, provided he could keep up to us.

We were anxious as soon as possible to hand our prisoners over to the police, lest their two comrades, still at large, with others of the gang they might fall in with, should attempt their rescue; but we felt pretty secure, as they would know that, so long as we were on the watch, they were not likely to succeed. Should we, however, be kept out another night, they would compel us to be very vigilant, while we should have to guard both ourselves and the horses.

Although the two bushrangers had escaped, we had succeeded in breaking up the gang, and without guns and ammunition they would have great difficulty in supporting themselves; while the two we had made prisoners would probably, on their trial, be ready to give such information as might assist in the capture of others.

Leading on our prisoners, we now set out to return to where we had left the dominie.

We had, I should have said, hurriedly eaten some of the provisions Guy and Hector had cooked, and we took the remainder so that no time need be lost in proceeding to Bracewell's.

On reaching the spot, what was our dismay to see neither the dominie nor the horses. We shouted to him, but no reply came.

"What can have become of him?" exclaimed Guy. "Those fellows must have fallen in with him, and compelled him to accompany them."

"I do not think that is possible," I remarked, "for they went off in a different direction. Still his disappearance is very mysterious. We must try to learn what the black thinks about the matter."

We inquired of our guide, by signs and such words as he understood.

He examined the ground on every side and then started off at a run in a southerly direction, and on closer examination we discovered traces of the horses.

After waiting some time, as the black did not return, Guy proposed that Hector should stay by the prisoners and the two animals we had recovered, while he and I went in search of our missing friend.

Hector undertook to do as proposed.

"I'll hobble all four of them," he observed, "and there'll be no risk of their getting away."

Not wishing to lose more time we started. After going on for some time we got separated, and I found to my right a deep gully, with steep cliff-like banks, mostly covered with trees of a character which showed that there was generally an abundance of water; indeed, I observed several small pools, joined by a trickling rivulet three or four feet only in width.

As I went along, I shouted out our friend's name. At last I heard the tramp of horses, and looking about, I caught sight through the trees of our two animals with their saddles on their backs, the black following, driving them before him.

I was thankful to find that they had been recovered, though much grieved not to see the dominie, for I naturally feared that some serious accident had happened to him. I now once more returned, intending to rejoin Hector, when I heard a faint shout. It came from the direction of the gully. My hopes revived of finding the dominie. After going on some way, I again heard the shout followed by a cooey which I was sure, however, was not uttered by him. It was the voice either of Guy or Hector.

I cooeyed in return. Soon afterwards another reached my ears, coming from the same direction. At last I gained the summit of a cliff, when, looking down, I saw Guy bending over the prostrate form of a man.

I soon joined my brother, and found that the fallen person was the dominie. Guy was employed in chafing his hands, and trying to restore him to consciousness.

"Can he have been attacked by bushrangers, and thrown here?" I asked.

"I don't think that," answered Guy, pointing up to the cliff. "See, he must have fallen over, and striking his head on the ground, have become insensible. Go and get some water from yonder pool in your hat, and I think that if we bathe his head, he will come to."

I did as Guy desired me, and in a short time we had the satisfaction of seeing our companion revive.

"Have you got the horses?" were the first words he spoke.

"All right!" I answered, "and we have captured two bushrangers into the bargain."

The news seemed to have a good effect, and now that he had come to himself, he quickly, with our assistance, was able to get up the cliff, when we helped him along.

In a short time we joined Hector, who had caught the horses driven up to him by the black.

We immediately mounted, and Hector taking charge of one prisoner, and Guy of the other, I attended to the dominie. We expected that our black guide would have kept up with the horses, but when he found the rate at which we went, he appeared to have had enough of our society, and, suddenly bolting off into the bush, disappeared.

"It is the way of those black fellows," observed Hector. "He has obtained more than he expected, and has no fancy to be shot by the bushrangers, should we encounter them; probably, also, he wants to join his gins, who, I dare say, are not far off, though they have kept out of our sight."

We rode on, when the ground was level breaking into a gallop. The dominie now and then groaned, but when I offered to pull up, he always answered—

"Go on, go on; perhaps those villains will be

watching for us; I don't want to be stuck up again or shot."

When I observed that they had only pistols, he answered—

"Ah, well! pistols will kill as well as rifles, and we don't know at what moment they may pounce out from this thick scrub."

As I thought it possible that they might make an attempt to surprise us, I was not sorry to follow the dominie's wishes.

We made such good way that I hoped we should reach Bracewell's before sundown. Late in the day, I began to recognise spots we had passed while staying with him, although so great is the sameness of the country, that I could not feel very certain that such was the case, until I heard Guy, who was ahead, sing out—

"Here we are! I see the top of Bracewell's hut."

We gave a cooey to let those at the station know of our approach, and in another moment old Bob came hurrying out to meet us.

"Thankful you've come, gentlemen," he exclaimed; "though Mr. Bracewell's round the corner, he'll be glad of your society. He's in terribly low spirits at having only me to look after him. But, whom have you there? Picked up a couple of pirates on the road?"

We soon explained who our captives were. Old Bob shook his fist at them.

"You rascals! You're caught at last, are you? You'll be having your legs in chains before long I

"GUY BENDING OVER THE PROSTRATE FORM OF A MAN." [*p*. 118

hope, and not be keeping honest folk in fear of their lives."

"We must see where we can stow these fellows until we can send for the police," said Guy.

"We'll stow them safe enough," said old Bob, "and, provided we keep their arms lashed behind their backs, and their legs in limbo, they'll not escape from where I'll put them."

The captive bushrangers cast angry glances at the speaker, but as their mouths were still gagged, they could not express their feelings by words.

Before we went in to see Bracewell, we had hauled them off their horses, and under Bob's directions, dragged them into a hut, which had only one door and one window. He then brought a couple of stout ropes, with which we secured them to the posts which supported the roof, one on either side of the hut, so that they could not reach each other. We next drew the gags from their mouths, expecting that they would make the first use of their tongues by abusing us, but they appeared to be too dull and brutal even to do that. After closing the door and window, we left them to their own devices.

"I'll take care that they don't get out during the night. If they try that dodge, I'll send a bullet through their heads," muttered old Bob.

Bracewell, who had been asleep when we arrived, awoke as we entered, delighted to see us, and insisted on getting up to do the honours of his hut. Old Bob in the meantime was cooking supper, and a very satisfactory one he managed to produce.

Our coming, as we expected, did our friend a great

deal of good, and we hoped that the medicine which the dominie brought would still further restore him.

Old Bob insisted that a guard should be kept on the prisoners, and he offered to stand watch for four hours, provided we three took the remainder of the night between us. To this we could not object, though when he aroused me, I confess that I got up very unwillingly.

I was thankful, however, that his advice was followed. While standing before the door, I heard one of the fellows announce to his comrade that he had got one of his arms free, and that in another minute he would set him at liberty. Had they succeeded in doing this, they would have had no difficulty in working their way out of the hut.

I at once opened the door, and walked up to the fellow with a pistol in my hand. I found that he had really managed to get an arm free, though the moment he saw me he placed it behind him.

I shouted to old Bob, who quickly came to my assistance, and we soon had the fellow more securely fastened than before. We then examined the other. Though he had evidently been trying his best to get out his arms, he had not succeeded. As may be supposed, we did not allow them an opportunity of attempting the same trick again, and when I called up Guy, I charged him to keep a watch on the two fellows, a lantern being placed in the middle of the hut to throw its light upon them.

At daybreak Hector rode off to execute the commissions for his father, and at the same time to summon the police.

As our prisoners required our constant attention, we were very thankful when a dozen black troopers came clattering up to the station under the command of an English officer, to whom we handed over the bushrangers, and gave a full description of how they had been caught, and of their two companions who had escaped.

We had, as we expected, to go and give evidence; but, fortunately, as their trial came on at once, we were not long delayed.

By the time we were wanted, Bracewell, thanks to the dominie's medical skill, had almost entirely recovered. He was able to identify the two men as among the party who had attacked him, we also having found in their possession some of his property which they had taken. The other two were still at large, but the police entertained no doubt that they should catch them before long.

We all returned to Bracewell's, and I was glad to find that he had accepted an invitation from Mr. Strong, to pay him a visit, which he was able to do as he had engaged a trustworthy man to assist old Bob in taking care of the station. We therefore prepared to set out immediately.

CHAPTER VII.

WE were actually in our saddles and about to set off, when Hector received a letter from his father directing him to return to town to make some further purchases, and to transact other business.

The dominie, who had been expressing a wish to visit the city and buy some books, begged permission to accompany him.

"You go on leisurely, we'll soon catch you up," said Hector. "It is a pity that you should be delayed for us."

Bracewell agreed to this arrangement. As his strength was not completely restored, it was considered advisable that he should make short stages. While we therefore rode on as we intended to the north-west, our friends, borrowing a couple of horses, that their own might be fresh when they returned to the station, galloped off towards the coast.

We were approaching a water-hole by the side of which we proposed encamping the first evening, when we caught sight of a native walking leisurely along with an axe in his hand. He came forward with a confidence which showed that he was accustomed to meet white men, and we recognised, as he approached, our former guide. He appeared to be highly pleased at seeing us, and began jabbering away in a language which neither Guy nor I could understand. Bracewell, who seemed to comprehend him, replied in the same lingo; and then told us that the black had informed him that his tribe was in the neighbourhood and would be happy if we would pay them a visit, that they might show their gratitude for the wealth we had showered upon them.

While he was speaking, another black popped his head out from behind the bushes, when the other called to him, and he came forward. As he was approaching he cast his eyes to the top of a tree, a little distance off, when a few words were exchanged between the two.

They both ran to it and without more ado, began to ascend, cutting slight notches with their axes, just of sufficient size to enable them to put in their toes and fingers.

We watched their proceedings with wonder at the rapidity with which they got up, almost indeed as fast as if they were mounting an ordinary ladder. Round and round the tree they climbed, giving a couple of strokes with their little axes sufficient to make a notch of the required size. Until I saw the confidence with which they proceeded, I expected every moment that they would drop down again to the ground. Though the tree must have been sixty feet high without a branch, they were at the top in less than a minute, when securing themselves they plunged down their hands. While the one drew out an opossum, the other, before the animal could bite him, knocked it on the head and threw it to the ground.

They descended with even greater celerity than they had mounted, and then to our surprise brought the animal to us, apparently as an offering.

Bracewell thanking them, told them to keep it for themselves, which they were evidently well content to do. They accompanied us to the water-hole, where, without being told to do so, they assisted in collecting sticks for a fire.

This being done, we having hobbled our horses, they squatted themselves on the ground to skin their opossum which they then brought to be roasted. The confidence they exhibited in us showed that we might trust them, and we allowed them to go about the camp as they liked, though Bracewell advised that we should keep an eye on our saddle-bags and valises lest the temptation to appropriate their contents might be too great to be resisted.

While we were discussing our supper, they managed to devour the whole of the opossum between them; and then, having stuck some boughs in the ground to form a hut, they lay down side by side beneath them, and were quickly asleep, evidently feeling perfectly secure in our neighbourhood.

Both Guy and I wanted to see more of the natives, and Bracewell consented, should our guests again offer to guide us to their camp, to ride round to it, as it would not take us much out of our way. There was, he said, a few miles off, a large shallow lagoon, near which they were assembled for the purpose of fishing and catching the wild fowl which frequented

"ROUND AND ROUND THE TREE THEY CLIMBED." [p. 127.

it; and that we should thus have an opportunity of seeing the way in which they engaged in those pursuits. As he knew the country well, he could easily make his way back to the direct route, so that we could run no risk of missing Hector and the dominie. That Bracewell might enjoy a full night's rest, Guy and I agreed to keep watch and watch, but he laughed at our proposal, declaring that it was useless.

"But should bushrangers stumble upon us, we might all three be stuck up, and find ourselves minus our horses and rifles," said Guy.

"No chance of that," answered Bracewell, "the fellows were certain to clear out of this part of the country, when they knew the police were on their tracks. There is a greater risk from the blacks, though I feel sure those two fellows there can be trusted."

In spite of Bracewell's remarks, Guy and I determined to keep to our resolution, and as soon as he was asleep, I rose, and having made up the fire, walked about, endeavouring to keep my eyes open. I tried this for some time, when feeling tired, I sat down with my rifle by my side.

How it was I could not tell, but before long I found myself stretched on the ground, and when I awoke the fire was almost out. Giving a kick to the embers to obtain a flame, I looked at my watch. It was then almost day-break and I thought it useless to rouse my brother. Directly afterwards a chorus of cachinnations from a couple of laughing jackasses, gave me notice that the morning would soon commence.

I called Guy and Bracewell, who shrewdly suspected what had happened, although as no harm had come of it, they spared me any severe remarks.

While we were breakfasting, the blacks, who had got on their legs, sauntered up to the camp, and begged for some of the tea and damper on which we were regaling ourselves.

To catch our horses, saddle up and mount, did not take us long, and as our new friends repeated their offer, we set off, the blacks running ahead. As they were making their way through scrub some distance ahead, one of them stopped and called to the other, when they each cut a long thin switch and ran towards an object which we just then saw moving in the grass. Presently the wicked-looking head of a large snake rose in the air. The blacks ran towards it, one on either side, and bestowing some sharp blows with their wands, down it dropped. On getting up to the spot, we found that it was a snake between nine and ten feet long.

The blacks seemed to consider it a great prize, for, chopping off the head, one of them slung the body over his shoulder, and they then again went on shouting with glee.

In a short time we arrived at the blacks' camp. It consisted of a number of rude bowers, such as I have before described, tenanted by a few women, children, and old men, all the active men being out hunting in the lagoon which appeared just beyond.

Riding on we caught sight of a number of black figures, scattered in all directions, engaged in knocking down with their boomerangs some large birds perched on the withered branches of the trees overhanging the water.

Our friends brought us one of the boomerangs to examine. It was a curved piece of wood about two feet two inches from tip to tip, rather more than two inches wide in the middle, and diminishing towards the tips.

We saw bird after bird knocked off the trees with this remarkable weapon. When it first left the hand of the thrower, we could not decide in what direction it was going, but after making numberless circles in the air, it never failed to hit the object intended.

Most of the birds we saw struck were cormorants, which, as they fell into the water, the blacks seized and wrung their necks. Some, however, not being killed outright or stunned, showed fight, and attacked the naked bodies of their assailants with their sharp beaks. We witnessed the sport for some time, till the birds nearest us becoming alarmed, took to flight, but were followed by the persevering hunters, who marked where they again alighted.

As we did not wish to delay, we thanked our friends, who with the prospect of an ample feast before them, showed no inclination to accompany us. One of them, however, had a talk with Bracewell just before we started.

"What was the black fellow saying?" I asked as we rode along.

"He told me that a mob of bad black fellows, as he called them, are in the neighbourhood, and that we must take care not to fall in with them, as they will not scruple to spear our horses at night, or, should we be off our guard, murder us."

"What had we better do then?" I enquired.

"Be on our guard and not let them surprise us," he answered, laughing. "I have no fear of the blacks, provided they know that we are prepared to give them a warm reception. We will, however, keep a look-out for the fellows, and as soon as we get back to the regular track, I'll leave a note fixed to a tree for Hector, telling him what we have heard, and advising him and the dominie to keep a watch at night on their horses, as I don't think it's worth while waiting for them.

"Still, notwithstanding what our black friend said, the chances are that we shall not fall in with the mob of bad natives," he added; and as he knew the country much better than Guy or I did, we were perfectly ready to be guided by his opinion.

We soon again got into the main track.

On reaching it, Bracewell taking out his pocket-book, wrote a few lines, warning Hector that a mob of blacks were said to be in the neighbourhood, and telling him where we proposed camping.

Cutting some thorns, he pinned it to a tree in a conspicuous place.

"Hector will not fail to observe it," he said, as he did so.

"But if the blacks see it they'll tear it down surely," I remarked.

"They'll not do that," he answered, "they'll fancy it is some charm, and will not venture to touch it."

This done, we pushed forward, rather faster than

we had hitherto been going, in order to arrive at a spot at which Bracewell advised that we should camp early in the evening.

Although there were several stations scattered over the country in various directions, the traffic between them was so limited, that no inns or even liquor stores had been established; and travellers had consequently to camp out in the bush night after night when proceeding towards the interior.

We found doing this was no hardship, and infinitely preferred sleeping by our camp fire with the canopy of heaven above us, to taking up our quarters in a shepherd's hut or grog shop.

We were approaching the end of our day's journey, when I caught sight of a black figure flitting among the trees in the distance. Presently another, and another appeared. They did not come near us, but were apparently moving in the same direction that we were.

I pointed them out to Bracewell.

"I saw the rascals," he answered. "They are up to mischief very likely, and think it prudent to keep at a distance from us. I'll soon make them vanish."

Lifting his rifle, he uttered a loud whoop, when in an instant every black disappeared, either having dropped to the ground, or got behind the stems of trees.

"I don't suppose they'll come near us again, but it will be as well to be on our guard when passing any thick scrub. We must either give it a wide berth so that their spears cannot reach us, or gallop quickly by."

During the day-time, however, there was not much probability that the blacks would venture to attack us; but we agreed that we must be very careful during the night, lest they should spear our horses,—a trick they are apt frequently to play when they think that they can do so and make their escape without the risk of a bullet through their bodies.

Though we looked out for them on every side, not another black did we see; but Bracewell remarked, that we must not consequently fancy that they had taken themselves off.

However, as the day wore on, and they did not again reappear, we began to hope that we had distanced them, and that they would not trouble us during the night. At length we reached the water-hole, near which grew several magnificent trees, where there was abundance of grass for the horses, so that they would not be tempted to stray away.

Choosing a spot with a water-hole on one side, and three or four fine trees of large girth on the other, we unsaddled our horses and made up our fire. We had provisions enough for the evening, but should have to go on short commons the next day, unless we could shoot a paddy melon or some birds.

Bracewell offered, as there was still sufficient light, to try to do so; but Guy and I advised him to remain in camp while we endeavoured to shoot a few parrots or cockatoos, so many of which were flitting about among the boughs that we felt confident of shooting as many as we required.

No sooner, however, did we fire, than having each brought down a parrot, the remainder of the noisy

"KNOCKING DOWN WITH THEIR BOOMERANGS SOME LARGE BIRDS." [*p.* 132.

birds flew away. We followed, expecting to get some more shots, but the sound of our guns having alarmed them, as soon as we approached they again took to flight.

By some means or other, I, having hurried on, lost sight of Guy, though I concluded that he was following me. At last I saw a large cockatoo nodding his head as if not aware of my presence. I fired, and brought him down, when directly afterwards I heard the report of Guy's gun, much further off than I had expected.

The thought just then occurred to me, that should the blacks be in the neighbourhood, they might discover our whereabouts by the reports; so I felt that it would be wise to be satisfied with the birds we had killed, and return to camp.

I was therefore making my way back, when, turning my head, I caught sight of a black figure stealthily approaching with a lance in his hand. Suspecting that his intentions were hostile, I quickly reloaded, ramming down a ball. As he approached from behind the trunk of a tree, I levelled my rifle. He vanished in an instant, though when I moved on again, I felt pretty sure that he was following me. I therefore every now and then turned suddenly round and pointed my rifle towards my pursuer. At last, having gone on for some distance, I began to fear that I had lost my way, for I could not see either our camp-fire or the smoke rising from it. To ascertain if I was near it, I gave a loud cooey, expecting that Guy and Bracewell would hear me and reply.

No answer came. I began to feel rather uncomfortable, for although with my rifle in my hand, I was a match for two or three blacks, I should be in an awkward predicament should I be followed by a whole mob. It would not do to stop, so on I pushed.

Again I cooeyed, and this time I heard my friends cooey in return. Still the distance was apparently considerable, and at any moment the blacks might overtake me. I ran on as fast as the nature of the ground would allow, endeavouring to keep a straight course.

Once more I turned round when to my dismay I beheld a score or more of blacks armed with spears and shields. For a moment I faced them as before, presenting my rifle. I might bring down one of the fellows, I knew; but then, unarmed, I should be at their mercy; I therefore contented myself with threatening them. The instant I raised my weapon, they all vanished as before. Directly afterwards I caught sight of the glare of the fire : I dashed forward, when to my surprise I found my brother and Bracewell coolly seated on the ground, engaged in preparing a couple of parrots which the former had shot.

"Up, up!" I exclaimed: "the blacks are upon us—there is not a moment to lose if we intend to save our lives."

"Oh, nonsense!" cried Bracewell. "You've seen a big 'boomer,' or the stump of a tree, which you have mistaken for a black fellow."

I loudly protested that I was not mistaken, and advised them to load their rifles with ball.

While I was speaking, a spear quivered in the tree

close to where they were sitting. They jumped to their feet in an instant.

"If we don't take care, we shall have the horses wounded," I exclaimed, and I ran to where they were feeding, leaving Guy and Bracewell to keep watch for the appearance of our enemies.

Just as I had brought the horses up, and was tethering them behind the clump of trees, the mob of blacks came in sight, shrieking and dancing and brandishing their spears.

Bracewell, on this, exclaimed, "We'll show them that we're not to be trifled with; or they will become bolder, and make a rush upon us with their waddies. Guy, do you pick off that fellow on the right; I'll take the fellow in the centre who is flourishing his weapon —he intends to hurl it at us as soon as he gets near enough. Maurice, you must keep them in check while we are reloading, but don't fire unless they advance."

As he spoke, he and Guy pulled their triggers. As the smoke cleared off I saw two blacks on the ground —my companions were rapidly reloading while I kept my rifle pointed at the advancing mob. I had my eye upon one of them, who appeared to be leader. We were tolerably well sheltered by the roots of the trees, so that we could take aim without exposing ourselves.

The determined front we exhibited did not however deter the blacks from advancing, and as they did so, they sent a whole shower of spears, which stuck quivering in the trunk of the tree forming our chief protection. Several, however, passed and fell into the ground close to the horses, fortunately none of which were injured.

I fired and brought down the man at whom I had aimed; I then sprang behind shelter and reloaded, while my brother and Bracewell knocked over two more.

It was dreadful work, having thus to kill our fellow-creatues; but at that moment all we thought about was that they intended to kill us, and that it was our business to defend our lives. Whether or not we should do so successfully seemed very doubtful; for as far as we could judge, while they flitted in and out among the trees, there were a hundred or more of them yelling and shrieking and hurling their sharp-pointed spears towards us. A hundred opposed to three were fearful odds. Probably they were not aware of the smallness of our number, or they might have made a rush at our camp, and knocked us all over with their waddies. Every moment we expected that they would do so. Should one of us be killed or wounded so as to be unable to fire, the other two must inevitably become their victims.

As yet we had happily escaped injury, and the blacks did not appear inclined to venture closer than at first. We had been firing away as rapidly as we could reload, but though we had killed several, we had frequently missed, for as they kept springing in and out behind the trees in the thickening gloom, it was very difficult to hit them. Suddenly they vanished, and I was afraid were coming round to get on our flank; the width of the water-hole, and the marshy ground on the further side was, however, too great to allow them to hurl their spears across it. My gun was loaded, but when I put my hand into my bullet-pouch, to my dismay, I found that I had not another shot left. I told my companions. "Neither have I, and have just loaded with small shot," said Bracewell.

"So have I," said Guy; "but it will do to pepper them with if they come nearer."

"But small shot will not go through their shields," I remarked.

"Then we must aim at their legs," answered Bracewell, calmly.

"Don't you think it would be prudent to mount the horses and gallop off before they again attack us?" asked Guy.

"They will probably be on the look-out should we make the attempt, and surround us before we get to any distance," said Bracewell. "Better try and hold our own here, where we have the shelter of the trees, only don't throw a shot away."

This discussion was cut short by a loud yell uttered by our savage enemies, who, the next instant, again came into view, and advanced with their spears poised. We had barely time to spring behind the trees, when a shower of spears flew through the air, some passing close to us, others sticking in the opposite side of the trunks. We immediately replied, but could not see whether our shots took effect. The spears now fell so thickly, that we could scarcely venture to show ourselves even for a moment to fire in return. By the sound of the savages' voices we judged they were getting nearer, and now we all felt that we should have to sell our lives dearly, unless we could manage to mount our horses and gallop away; but it would take some time to saddle them, and the natives were not likely to allow us many moments to do so. Bracewell, however, desperate as was our condition, tried to keep up our spirits.

As far as we could judge, the savages showed no intention of abandoning their object. Just as we expected that they would make their final rush, a loud cooey was heard, and I caught the sound of the trampling of horses' feet. We cooeyed in return again and again. The savages must have heard us, as well as the cooeys in the distance; for after vainly hurling another shower of spears, they turned and scampered off as fast as their legs could carry them, their flight hastened by the peppering we gave their backs with small shot. Almost immediately afterwards Hector and the dominie, accompanied by half a dozen troopers, came galloping up along the path close to the water-hole. As they appeared, without waiting to exchange words, we threw our saddles on our horses' backs and mounted ready to join them in the pursuit of our foes.

CHAPTER VIII.

THE sergeant in command of the troopers told us that they had been sent forward in search of some bushrangers who with unaccountable hardihood, notwithstanding the capture of two of their companions, were still committing their depredations in that part of the country; and that having accompanied Hector, who had discovered our note, they had come on to assist us in case we should be attacked by the blacks.

We all rode on together in the direction we supposed the savages to have taken. But darkness was coming on: the sergeant soon pulled up declaring that we might as well look for a needle in a bundle of hay, as expect to catch one of them.

Had we had any natives with us we might have tracked them during the night. We should now however only run the risk of losing our way without the slightest chance of capturing a black man.

This was very evident, and we accordingly settled to return to the camp and wait until the following morning.

Hector and the dominie had brought a good supply of provisions in their saddle-bags, and our supper being cooked, we sat round the fire sipping our mugs of scalding tea, and fighting our battle over again.

The sergeant told us that the mob which had attacked us was said to be the most daring in that part of the country. They had already, it was supposed, murdered two hut-keepers and a shepherd, and had carried off large numbers of sheep. Without natives to track them it would be impossible to come upon their camp so as to capture their leaders. The punishment they had received from us might perhaps, we thought, prevent them from committing further depredations in the neighbourhood; and the sergeant's business for the present was to hunt down the bush-rangers, which was more in his way. He, as soon as he had seen us safely on our road, must continue his course in the direction he had been informed they had taken.

At length we began to get drowsy, and one after the other we lay down with our horse-cloths for bedding and our saddles for pillows.

The sergeant undertook that one of his men should keep watch, though it was very improbable that the blacks would venture to attack us during the night.

I was awakened just before dawn by the "settler's clock," as the laughing-jackass is frequently called; and lifting my head, by the light of the still burning embers of our fire saw the dominie rubbing his eyes, but no one else was moving. I suspected from this that the last man on guard had gone to sleep. No sticks had been thrown on for a considerable time, and on counting heads I discovered that the sergeant and his troopers were all snoring loudly, and sound asleep. I bethought me that we would play them a trick; so quickly arousing Guy and Bracewell, I proposed that we should unite our voices and give a terrific shriek as if a whole mob of black fellows were about to break into the camp. They agreed.

We did shriek with a vengeance, the echo resounding through the forest. The effect was electrical. Up jumped the sergeant and his men and seizing their arms prepared to receive their expected foes.

"Whereabouts are they?" exclaimed the sergeant. "Reserve your fire, until you see them," he added—a caution I should not have considered necessary. "Did any of you gentlemen catch sight of them?" he asked.

Our loud laugh told him the trick we had played.

"Which of you lads was keeping guard?" he enquired.

"I was," answered one, who had been among the loudest of the snorers, and we found that the speaker had in reality the middle watch, but having dropped off, had not called his relief.

We thought it best to say as little as possible about the matter, for according to strict military discipline, the man who goes to sleep on guard in the face of an enemy, becomes liable to the punishment of death. The sergeant also, who was a good-natured fellow, was evidently anxious not to take too much notice of the matter.

We soon got the fire made up, and having breakfasted, we mounted and rode in the direction we supposed that the blacks had taken, but except the dead bodies of the men we had shot, no trace of them could we discover. They probably could not tell whether or not we had any natives with us, and therefore took care to leave no trail by which they could be followed up. They might possibly have been hiding all the time in the neighbourhood, or might—contrary to their usual custom—have travelled during the night.

After looking for an hour or more we agreed that it would be useless to search further and pursued our course towards Mr. Strong's. The sergeant's way for some distance lay in the same direction, and he and his men therefore accompanied us. We had got about half way, when we saw a white man running towards us. He appeared to be in a desperate hurry, and as he approached made signs entreating us to stop.

"What's the matter, my man?" inquired Bracewell as he came up.

"I am a shepherd on Mr. Robinson's out-station," he answered. "I had driven my flock to the run this morning, when who should I see coming towards me but old Bill the hut-keeper who had a spear in his side and another in his back. He had just time to tell me that, soon after I had gone, a whole mob of blacks surrounded the hut, and to the best of his belief were still either in or about it, when, though I did my best to help him by cutting out the spear, he sank back and died. On this I was afraid to stay where I was lest the blacks should find me out, and was trying to reach Mr. Strong's or some other station, when I saw you."

This account made us resolve at once to try and surprise the blacks. The shepherd acknowledged that he and his mate had just before got in on the sly some

"SOON HAD SEVERAL SECURED BY THEIR NECKS." [*p*. 152.

bottles of rum, which it was possible the blacks might have found; and that if so, should we advance cautiously, we might very likely catch them. Not a moment however was to be lost, and one of the troopers taking the shepherd up behind him on his horse to act as our guide, we set off in the direction of the hut. It was so situated at the bottom of a hill, with a belt of trees on one side, that led by the shepherd we were able to get close up to it without being discovered.

We there dismounted, leaving our horses under the charge of the dominie who volunteered for the service.

We crept cautiously down towards the hut, the sounds proceeding from which showed us to our great satisfaction, that it was still in possession of the blacks. We now advanced with greater caution, Bracewell and Hector, who were the most experienced in bush life, leading, I following, until we could look right down upon the hut. A few blacks were squatting on the ground outside, and the hut itself appeared to be full of them. The sergeant and his men, I should have said, had brought some coils of rope with which to bind any prisoners they might capture. These they formed into lassoes for the purpose of throwing over the heads of the blacks. As we watched the hut, the people collected round it had, as far as we could judge, no intention of moving, probably fancying that they were safe, for the present, from pursuit.

Bracewell now made a sign to us to rise to our feet, so that we might rush down on the hut and capture all the blacks in it if not those outside. At the signal we were in motion, the troopers with their drawn swords in one hand and their pistols in the other, and we with our rifles. We had got half way down the slope before the blacks discovered us. Most of those outside scampered off, but we saw, by the crowd at the door, that the hut was full, and before many could escape, we were at the entrance. Some tried to get out of the window on one side of the hut, but Guy, Hector, and I shot them down as they reached the ground, thus putting a stop to any others escaping in that direction; while the sergeant and his troopers, bursting into the hut, soon had several of the rest secured by their necks. Others were knocked down. The greater number either lay helpless on the ground or stared stupidly at their assailants. Had our object been slaughter we might have killed the whole mob, but the sergeant had received orders to capture as many as possible alive, and we were thankful not to have to destroy any more of the poor wretches.

Altogether, thirty were made prisoners, but we could not calculate how many had made their escape. The greater number, however, had left their spears and waddies behind them, so that they were not likely for the present to attempt further mischief. At the request of the sergeant we brought down the horses and assisted him in securing the prisoners and arranging them in the order in which they were to march. It took some time to bind the unfortunate wretches, whom we secured with their arms behind them, and then fastened together by strong ropes six in a line. Our next care was to collect all the arms, which, with the exception of a few we desired to possess, were broken and thrown on the fire.

There was very little chance of rescue; indeed, had the blacks still at liberty made the attempt, they would to a certainty have hastened the death of their friends. The shepherd entreated us to assist him in bringing in the body of the hut-keeper—a task, from a sense of humanity, we undertook, while he remained to look after his sheep.

We accordingly brought the body in on the dominie's horse and placed it in the bunk in which the unfortunate man, a few hours before, had been sleeping, little dreaming of the fate awaiting him. The dominie, Guy, and I remained at the hut, while Bracewell and Hector rode off to the head station to give information of what had occurred and to obtain a companion for the poor man.

Finding a couple of spades in the hut, Guy and I employed our time in burying the blacks who had been shot on the first onslaught. It was a far from pleasant undertaking, but it was better to put them underground before they were discovered by the dingoes or vultures, which would before long find them out.

The day was waning and as our companions had not returned we began to fear that we should have to spend the night in the hut. I was glad at length when I saw the shepherd returning with the flock. He thanked us heartily for what we had done.

When he entered the hut he seemed dreadfully upset at the sight of his dead mate. "It is a trying life, this shepherding, gentlemen," he observed; "with the chance of being speared or clubbed by the black-fellows, or stuck up by a bushranger, while one has to spend day after day without a human being to speak to, from sunrise to sunset—and then to have one's only chum killed so suddenly! It is well-nigh more than I can bear."

It was late at night before Bracewell and Hector came back, accompanied by Mr. Platt, the overseer from the head station, and another man to take the place of the murdered hut-keeper. As it was now too late to think of proceeding on our journey that night, we turned our horses into a spare paddock, where they could find grass enough to satisfy their hunger until the morning.

Having stowed our baggage inside the hut, after supper we lay down, where we could find room on the ground; one of the party, however, keeping watch in case the blacks should return, though it was not at all likely they would do that.

Before sunrise the shepherd and his new mate got up to dig a grave for the murdered man, in which we saw him placed before we started. We then, having breakfasted, continued our route, Mr. Platt accompanying us, as, for a couple of miles or so, our roads lay in the same direction. He had come away without his rifle, or arms of any description, excepting his heavy riding-whip, and he declared that they were unnecessary; for the blacks, he said, would never venture to attack a well-mounted man, and as for bushrangers, when there was no booty to be obtained they were not likely to interfere with him. He had ridden about the country in all directions, and except when hunting a kangaroo or emu, he had never had to fire a shot.

"But with a mob of savage blacks in the neighbourhood, it would be more prudent to be armed," I observed.

"My horse-whip will soon send them to the right-about, should any of them venture to come near me," he answered laughing. "However we have got half a dozen rifles at the head station, and as soon as I get back I'll arm each man and we'll quickly drive the remainder of the mob from the neighbourhood. Depend upon it if any are remaining they'll clear out fast enough when they find we are after them."

We soon got over the two miles the overseer was to accompany us. He then, thanking us for the service we had rendered his people, turned off to the right. He was still in sight, when we heard him shout, and I saw that he was galloping along with uplifted whip as if to strike some object on the ground. Supposing that he had called us, we rode towards him. Just then I saw a tall black man spring up from behind a bush and, with axe in hand, attack the overseer, who, it appeared to me, was in great danger of being killed; but as the savage was about to strike, the lash of the whip caught his arm and wrenched the weapon out of his hand.

The black, uttering a cry of disappointed rage, bounded away and a moment after was lost to sight among the scrub. On getting near to Platt we saw two more natives on the ground, the one a youth badly wounded, the other a gin, old and wrinkled, apparently the mother of the lad.

"I would not have attempted to strike them, had I seen that one was a woman and that the lad was wounded," said the overseer, as he pointed to the wretched beings; "but I fancied they were black fellows hiding away, and trying to escape my notice. The man who attacked me is probably the boy's father, and they have shown more than usual affection for their son."

"Don't you think that we could do something for the poor lad?" observed Bracewell. "Mr. Kimber will see what chance there is of his recovery."

"With all the pleasure in the world," said the dominie, dismounting, and he and Bracewell examined the lad's hurt.

The gin sat watching their proceedings.

"He is shot through the body. It is a wonder that he has lived so long, for I make no doubt he is one of the blacks who attacked the hut," observed the dominie. "I don't believe that the best surgeon in the land could do him any good. If we were to attempt to move him, he would die before we had carried him a hundred yards."

Bracewell expressed the same opinion.

We tried to make the old *gin* understand that there was no hope of her son's recovery; indeed, the next instant, while lifting him up, and after he had given a few gasps, his arms fell helplessly by his side, and we saw that he was dead.

"We had better leave him to his mother, and probably his father will return as soon as we have gone," observed Bracewell. "He has brought his fate upon himself, and we can do no more."

This was very evident, and the overseer, who was in a hurry to get back, galloped on, while we once more rode forward, leaving the poor woman with her dead son.

We had had enough of fighting, and were truly glad to reach Mr. Strong's station without any other accident. Bracewell was warmly welcomed. Although he had not before been a visitor at the house, his high character, his perseverance and industry were all known to Mr. Strong, who might possibly have had no objection to bestow upon him one of his blooming daughters.

We spent our time in the usual way, working on the station, varied with an occasional hunt after kangaroos, for as they eat up the grass required for the sheep, it is considered necessary to destroy them when they are numerous near a station. The blacks, after the severe lesson they had received from us, and from other settlers in the neighbourhood, betook themselves to another part of the country, and we had no longer any fear of being troubled by them.

We had been some days at Mr. Strong's, and Bracewell was talking of returning home, when a hut-keeper from the most distant station arrived in great alarm, stating that he had been beset the previous evening by a party of white men on horseback, who, taking his gun and ammunition, his week's supply of provisions and everything else. they could lay hands on in the hut, had lashed him hand and foot, threatening that if he gave information of their visit, they would return and kill him. Fortunately, soon after they had gone a shepherd arrived, but he had been afraid at first to leave the hut lest they should put their threat into execution. Waiting till daylight, he had followed their tracks for some distance, when he had hurried back to bring us information of the robbery. His idea was, that having supplied themselves with arms, they intended to pillage some of the larger stations, but how he arrived at this conclusion he did not say. His account was sufficiently clear to make us resolve to follow them up, and to try and put a stop to their career. Whether or not they were led by our former acquaintance, the big bushranger, and that unhappy fellow Vinson, we could not tell; but from the description the hut-keeper gave of two of the men who had attacked him, we strongly suspected that such was the case.

As there was no time to be lost, we at once organized a party to set out in search of the fellows. The only black on whom we could rely to act as a scout was our own attendant Toby, who volunteered, without hesitation, to accompany us. The party consisted of the three elder Strongs, Bracewell, Guy, and I, and two men from the station, with Toby. All of us were mounted, and we agreed to call on our way at Captain Mason's to get further reinforcements, thinking it not unlikely that the bushrangers had already paid him a visit, or if not that they were lurking in the neighbourhood.

As we rode fast we arrived at the captain's before the evening. He had seen nothing of the bushrangers; but we found the family somewhat in a state of alarm, as a shepherd had come in with the information that a keeper on one of the captain's stations had been killed in his hut the previous night, and that he himself had narrowly escaped with his life.

Captain Mason, therefore, gladly reinforced us with a couple of men; he, however, thinking it prudent to remain to defend his house, lest, during our absence, the daring ruffians might venture to attack it.

Riding towards the hut, we hoped that we might come upon the track of the outlaws. In this we were not mistaken; and Toby assured us that we should be able to follow them up, as they had taken no pains to conceal their movements. As it grew dark he dismounted, and led the way in a manner which showed that he was well accustomed to the work.

After going some distance, he begged us to halt, saying that we were not far off from the camp of the bushrangers.

Having pulled up under the shelter of some tall bushes, we waited to hear the report Toby might bring us. He again crept forward. We had not remained long, when the crack of a rifle was heard. As Toby had gone unarmed, with the exception of a long knife which he usually carried in his belt, we feared that coming suddenly on the bushrangers he had been shot. At all events, as concealment was no longer necessary, we dashed forward, Bracewell and I, with Mr. Strong's overseer leading. We had not gone far, when we caught sight of Toby standing with his knife in his hand, and, some twenty paces from him, of a man in the act of levelling his musket to fire.

That the latter was one of the bushrangers, there could be no doubt, and the overseer, without waiting to inquire, raising his rifle, discharged it. The bullet took effect, but not until the man had fired; Toby at the same moment fell to the ground, and I thought was killed; but the bushranger, before the smoke had cleared away, had darted behind a tree.

I had not fired, and my attention was attracted for an instant by Toby, who, to my great satisfaction, I saw spring to his feet and make chase after the fugitive. We called him back, thinking, probably, that the man was not alone, and that our black follower would fall a victim to his intrepidity; but, without heeding us, he dashed forward, and as soon as Bracewell had reloaded, we followed him. It was no easy matter, however, to make our way between the trees, which here grew unusually thick, while the ground was encumbered by fallen trunks and boughs. The spot had evidently been chosen by the bushrangers as a place likely to afford concealment, and, at the same time, enable them to defend themselves.

"That fellow was placed here on watch, to warn his comrades of the approach of an enemy, and, depend upon it, they are not far off," said Bracewell. "We shall come upon them presently, and it will be our own fault if we allow any of the gang to escape."

We now heard the sound of fire-arms, and as the bushrangers were warned of our approach, we knew that their first impulse would be to mount their horses and gallop off.

Our great object, therefore, was to prevent them from doing this, and unless they had kept their animals saddled and bridled, we had still a prospect of succeeding.

CHAPTER IX.

DARKNESS was coming on, but we had still light sufficient to see our way, and should we not come up with the bushrangers at once, they might be off, and we should find it a hard matter to overtake them. We had gone on for some minutes, expecting every instant to discover them, when Toby stopped.

"Dey dare," he said, pointing to a rocky knoll which rose just above the wood through which we were making our way. The reason they had not mounted their horses was now apparent, for we caught sight of the animals scampering away in the distance. The outlaws had probably taken up this position under the idea that they could effectually defend themselves against us, evidently not knowing the numbers composing our party. The instant we emerged from among the trees, several bullets came flying past our heads. By a simultaneous impulse we fired in return.

"On, on! before they have time to reload," cried Bracewell.

We dashed forward with our pistols in our hands. When we reached the knoll, not a man was to be seen on his feet, but three lay dead or dying among the rocks. At that instant a fourth sprang up with a rifle in his hand with which he was taking aim at Bracewell, when, before he had time to pull the trigger, the overseer fired and he fell. I had recognised Vinson, and as I rode up, I observed the look of agony and despair which overspread the countenance of my former school-fellow. I think he must have known me, but he was unable to speak, and before I could dismount he had ceased to breathe.

It was a sad end of a mis-spent life, and yet at one time Cyril Vinson was one of the most admired and sought after in a fashionable circle. Among the bodies we discovered that of the big bushranger, while we found that of the man who first fired a short distance from the knoll, where he had fallen and died before he had been able to reach his companions.

One of the gang only escaped, but Toby declined to go in search of him until the following morning, as he could not, he said, traverse the forest at night.

At daylight we followed him up, but found that he had managed to catch one of the horses, and for the time had made good his escape.

We got back to the station the next day. The information we brought of the destruction of the long dreaded gang, caused no small satisfaction to our neighbours. Some weeks afterwards the body of the bushranger who had escaped was discovered in a state of emaciation, showing that he must have been starved to death.

Although there is generally work enough on an Australian station to occupy everybody, we made frequent excursions to hunt kangaroo, dingoes, and

"TOBY STANDING WITH HIS KNIFE IN HAND." [p. 159.

emus. Mr. Strong, however, objected to the younger members of his family expending the large amount of powder and shot they were apt to fire away. He would allow them, he said, only the use of bows and arrows, promising, however, to give each a rifle when they could bring a parrot down on the wing, an emu running, or a kangaroo bounding over the ground. We therefore employed ourselves during the longer evenings of winter in manufacturing bows and feathering a large supply of arrows, for both of which objects we found suitable material.

We were in the meantime daily gaining experience in all farming operations which would prove of the greatest value when we should have charge of a station on our own account.

I had long promised to make a hunting trip with Hector and his two young brothers, Oliver and Ralph. As soon as our weapons were finished we set off, accompanied by Toby, who, since the courage he had displayed in capturing the bushrangers, had become a person of no small importance. I took the liberty, however, of carrying my rifle, as Hector also did his. We agreed to camp out for one or two nights, or as long as the flour and biscuits in our wallets would last.

It is usual to hunt the emu on horseback with dogs, when the bird is pursued until the dogs can get up to it, and seizing it by the throat drag it down. We, however, hoped with Toby's assistance to stalk it as the natives are in the habit of doing, and for this purpose our bows and arrows were likely to prove as efficient weapons as rifles, the report of which would be certain to drive the birds away from the spot where they were feeding; whereas the silent arrow might bring down one without frightening the others.

We tramped over many weary miles till we reached the edge of a large plain known to be frequented by emus, far beyond any of the sheep-runs. On one side it was bounded by an extensive scrub, which being fortunately to leeward, we hoped by creeping along under its cover to get within reach of the birds. We had proceeded some way when we caught sight of several, but they were all feeding too far off to give us any hope of shooting them without showing ourselves. Had we been mounted we might have been able to run down two or three, but being on foot, our best chance was to wait in ambush until some unwary bird got within range of our arrows. My idea was that, if we could shoot one, the others, from curiosity, would come to see what was the matter.

We accordingly agreed to wait patiently until we were certain of hitting our "quarry." Toby set us a good example by taking post behind a bush, where he stood looking like a bronze statue well blackened by London smoke.

Had two or three emus come near enough, I do not think that Hector and I could have resisted the temptation to use our rifles. Not a sound was heard, except when an emu uttered its hollow, booming note, as if carrying on a conversation with its mate. At length one of the noble birds came stalking up directly towards where we lay hid. It was fully seven feet in height, with powerful, stout legs, while its wings were so small that they could not be distinguished from its lightish brown and grey plumage. It got up to within twenty yards, when Oliver and Ralph, unable longer to restrain their eagerness, leapt to their feet, and sent a couple of shafts into its body. The emu, seeing them, turned tail, and off it went at a rapid rate. Influenced by a natural impulse, they started off in chase, instead of getting under cover and watching for the chance of another bird coming up to it. Toby also sprang out from behind a tree, and Hector and I followed, trusting that the arrows had struck deep enough, if not mortally to wound the emu, at all events, to prevent its keeping up the pace at which it was going. Our plucky young companions were fixing fresh arrows to their strings as they ran on, while Toby, bounding over the ground, promised soon to come up with the wounded bird. What had become of the other emus, I could not see; and I had to look where I was stepping, for fear of toppling down on my nose. I do not think I ever ran faster in my life. The emu kept on, but still it did not gain upon us sufficiently fast to make us abandon the hope of coming up with it. At length its pace became slower, and Oliver, who was leading, sent another arrow into its body. It went off again on feeling the pain, faster than ever; but before long, once more slackened its speed, though it still managed to keep ahead. A pretty long chase it led us altogether, still the excitement and prospect of catching it at last induced us to proceed, Oliver and Ralph shouting and hallooing in high glee, as they dashed over the ground, while Toby held his axe ready to give it a finishing blow as soon as he could get up to it. I was but a short distance behind the others, and supposed that Hector was following me; but at last the hard-pressed emu showed evident signs of giving in, and Oliver was springing towards it, when Toby shouted—

"Take care, him give kick one side!"

Fortunately Oliver followed this advice, when, in spite of its hurts, the bird struck out so furiously behind and on one side, that it would have broken his leg, or have inflicted a dangerous wound, had it struck him.

The black now, getting in front of it, threw the axe with so sure an aim, that the bird, its head almost cleft in two, fell dead to the ground.

The two boys uttered a shout of triumph, in which I joined. I expected to hear Hector's voice, but on looking round he was nowhere to be seen. What had become of him, neither his brothers nor the black could say. We were afraid that he must have hurt his foot, or fallen and been unable to follow. We could scarcely calculate how far we had come. Oliver declared that it must have been five miles at least; but I did not think the distance was nearly so much. The question was now, what to do with our emu while we went back in search of Hector, as we were unwilling to abandon so valuable a prize to the dingoes, who were very likely to find it out. Fortunately there were some bushes near which would afford fuel for a fire, and Toby consented to camp on the spot, while we returned to look for our companion.

I should have said that Guy and Bracewell had promised to ride after us the next morning with a

"A SAD END OF A MIS-SPENT LIFE." [*p.* 162.

spare horse or two, to carry back the spoils of the chase. I knew that they would come, although they had expressed great doubt whether we should have any game to carry home. They had settled to meet us at a spot with which Hector was acquainted; but if he were lost we should be unable to find it.

After we had taken some rest and food we set off, leaving Toby to skin and cut up the emu.

We had spent so much time in the chase, that it began to grow dark before we had got a mile on our way; still, as we had a compass with us, we were able to keep in the right direction.

"As the moon is about to rise, we shall soon be able to see our way," said Oliver; "but what can have happened to Hector?"

No one was able to answer that question. As we went on we shouted out his name, but no reply came, and I began to feel very uneasy. I thought that I had seen him certainly close to the point we had now reached.

I twice fired off my rifle, but listened in vain for the report of his. I now began to regret that we had not brought Toby with us, for he would have been far more likely to find him than we were.

His brothers were almost in despair.

"We had better go back and get Toby," exclaimed Oliver.

"Something dreadful must have happened. Perhaps he has been bitten by a poisonous snake, or kicked by an emu," said Ralph.

"Unless a mob of blacks have been hiding in the scrub and tracked us," I remarked.

"But then I don't see how they could have overtaken him without our seeing them," said Oliver.

At last it became so dark that we found it impossible to proceed, and it was proposed to halt until the moon should rise, when we should better be able to find our way.

We accordingly sat down on the ground to wait until the pale luminary of night could give us her light.

She rose even sooner than we had expected.

"Hurrah!" cried Oliver, "it will soon be almost as light as day, and unless Hector has fallen asleep, we shall find him."

We accordingly went on, shouting out as before. Presently my foot slipped into a hole, and I very nearly dislocated my ankle.

"What could have made that hole?" I exclaimed.

"Wombats, I've a notion," answered Oliver. "Look, there's one of the creatures!" As he spoke we saw an animal like a small bear waddling along over the ground. Presently we caught sight of another and another. We had evidently got into a colony of the creatures.

"I wonder we did not come across these when we were running after the emu," I observed. "I am afraid that we have got out of our way."

"We must have been close on one side or the other, for I'm certain that we were at no great distance from this," answered Oliver.

"Hector, Hector!" he shouted.

"Listen!" cried Ralph: "I heard a voice. It came from the right—it's not far off there!"

Again we shouted, when listening attentively we all three heard a reply and felt sure that we were not mistaken as to the direction from which it came.

On making our way towards the spot we caught sight of a dozen or more wombats, and presently of the head and arms of a person rising above the ground.

"That must be Hector! Hector, Hector, is it you?" shouted Oliver.

"Yes, yes! make haste or I shall tumble back again," was the answer.

We sprang forward and caught him by the arms; when, all three hauling away, we quickly dragged him out of a large hole into which he had fallen.

"Take care," he said. "I cannot stand—I sprained my ankle when falling into the hole, and the pain was so great that I believe I must have fainted. When I came to myself, I found that it was perfectly dark, and no sooner had I managed to reach the top of the hole than a whole herd of those wombats came sniffing round me, wondering what strange creature had got among them. I shouldn't have minded them, had they not tried to bite my hands and compelled me to let go again."

The wombats, on our appearance, had waddled off, so that they did not interfere with us while we were attending to Hector.

On his trying to use his foot he found that his ankle was not so much injured as he had supposed, and that by supporting himself on our shoulders he could manage to hobble along. He therefore very willingly agreed to try and get back to the camp.

"OLIVER AND RALPH SENT A COUPLE OF SHAFTS INTO ITS BODY." [*p.* 167.

"But what has become of your gun?" I asked; "can you remember where you left it?"

"I'm sure I don't know," answered Hector; "I had it in my hand when I fell, but when I felt about for it I could nowhere find it."

We searched for the rifle round the hole and at last came to the conclusion that it must have fallen in.

Ralph offered to descend.

He got down without difficulty and soon cried out that he had found the rifle at the bottom. "Stay, I have found something else," he added as he handed up the rifle. "While I was groping about, my hand came in contact with two hairy creatures. Here they are!" and stooping down again he hauled out two young wombats. We speedily knocked them on the head, agreeing that they would make a very good roast for supper.

We should have been puzzled to know how the big wombat got out of the hole, had not Ralph told us that he had found a passage sloping upwards to a smaller entrance some distance off.

As the two small wombats might not prove sufficient for all hands I shot a big fellow which measured nearly three feet in length, and was covered with a thick hairy coat.

Ralph undertook to carry it on his shoulders, while Oliver and I supported Hector.

We now lost no time in making our way back to the camp. Our progress was of necessity slow, but we reached it at last, having been guided during the latter part of the distance by the bright flames of Toby's fire.

We immediately set to work to cook the wombat. Toby however had satisfied his hunger on the flesh of the emu, though he managed after a little rest to devour no small portion of the meat we had brought.

We then lay down to sleep, pretty well tired by the fatigue we had gone through. To our dismay Hector was utterly unable to walk the next morning, but fortunately our friends discovered us on their way to the rendezvous, and he mounting one of the horses we set off for home. We carried with us the emu, which it was calculated would yield between six and seven quarts of fine oil. It is for the sake of this valuable product that the bird is generally hunted.

Hector very good-naturedly bore the bantering of the rest of the party on the subject of his adventure among the wombats.

We had ridden some distance across the open country, when we observed ahead what looked like a dense black mist in the far distance above the scrub.

"What can that be?" I asked of Bracewell.

"I don't like its appearance," he answered. "I fear that the bush is on fire, and if so it is impossible to say where it will stop. It appears to be at no great distance from the station. What do you think, Hector?"

"I'm sure it's very near," he answered hurriedly; "and during this dry weather the rapidity with which it spreads is extraordinary. Push on, all of you; don't mind me, I can be of no use with this lame foot, but you may still be in time to assist in saving our dear ones at home should the fire reach the house. Here, Maurice, do you mount my horse, and

"WE CAUGHT SIGHT OF THE HEAD OF A PERSON RISING ABOVE THE GROUND." [*p. 172.*

I'll get on the animal carrying the emu; there's not a moment to lose."

I willingly acted according to his suggestion; and, leaving him with his two younger brothers and Toby, Bracewell, Guy, and I galloped forward.

Bracewell appeared more agitated than I had ever seen him before. He had been paying great attention to Mary Strong, and the thought now occurred to him that she was in danger. While we were dashing on as hard as we could go, it appeared to us that the conflagration was rapidly extending. Already dense wreaths of smoke, rising towards the sky, formed a thick canopy overhead; while we could see every now and then the bright flames darting upwards above the intervening bush as some tall tree was wrapped in their embrace.

It was very evident that the homestead was in the greatest danger, even if it was not already encircled in flames; and although the inmates might have made their escape, we could not tell in what direction they had fled. They would have endeavoured to save as much of their property as possible from destruction, and Bracewell's fears conjured up the dreadful idea that they might have been caught by the rapidly advancing foe before they could reach a place of safety.

With whip and spur we urged on our animals. We had as yet seen no one to tell us in what direction our friends had gone. There was a stream to the left, used in the shearing season for washing the sheep, and Bracewell hoped that they might have made their way to it.

The intervening ground was free of trees, and the grass had been cropped so low that the fire was not likely to make much progress over it. They might, however, still be at the house, and towards it we directed our course.

As we galloped up what was our dismay to find it on fire, while the outbuildings were nearly burnt to the ground! We dashed up shouting to our friends, but no one replied.

"They must have gone across the stream," cried Bracewell; and turning our horses' heads we rode furiously on through the flames which had already caught the bushes on either side of us. After shouting again and again it was with unspeakable thankfulness that we heard our shouts answered, and dashing across the stream, we found the family assembled on a spot where the fire was not likely to reach.

Mary was on her palfrey, her father standing by her side endeavouring to quiet her alarm, while Mrs. Strong with the children and young people were seated on the ground among such articles as they had been able to save.

Our arrival greatly relieved their anxiety, for they had fancied that we and the boys might have been passing through a part of the wood in which the fire had been raging.

The flames spread to the east and the west, but having nothing to feed on near the stream they fortunately did not cross to the side on which we had taken refuge.

The fire continued to rage long after darkness had

WOMBATS.

come on, and grand and terrible was the spectacle it exhibited. We watched it anxiously not knowing how far it might extend. I was much struck with the calm way in which Mr. Strong endured his hard fortune. Not a murmur escaped his lips, but over and over again he expressed his gratitude to Heaven for having preserved all those dear to him from injury.

Under his directions we all turned to and put up some huts for the ladies, in which they passed the night. Mercifully towards morning a heavy fall of rain came on and extinguished the fire almost as suddenly as it had begun.

Next morning Mr. Strong set about ascertaining his losses and with wonderful energy took steps to repair them.

Bracewell invited the family to take up their abode at his hut until their new house was ready to receive them, and they immediately set off in one of the waggons which had escaped.

Guy and I, with the young Strongs, worked with the farm hands from morning till night, in putting up fences and rebuilding the house; and in a wonderfully short time the station, which had become little more than a mass of ruins, began to assume a habitable aspect.

Though we worked without wages the knowledge we gained was of the greatest value to us in our subsequent career. In a year or two our worthy cousin had completely recovered from the heavy losses he had sustained.

Bracewell before long became the husband of Mary Strong.

The proprietor of the next station to his wishing to sell out, we, assisted by him, were able to purchase it; and as soon as we had got up a tolerable residence, we sent to the old country for our mother and sisters; and I may honestly say we have had no cause to regret having fixed our home in Australia.

THE END.

W. H. G. KINGSTON'S
BOOKS OF TRAVEL AND ADVENTURE.

Price 5s. each, cloth.

GREAT AFRICAN TRAVELLERS: from Mungo Park to Livingstone and Stanley. A New Edition, brought down to the present time. With numerous Illustrations.

NOTABLE VOYAGES: from Columbus to Parry. With full-page Coloured Plates and many Illustrations. A New Edition, brought down to the present time.

SHIPWRECKS AND DISASTERS AT SEA. With numerous Illustrations.

Price 2s. 6d. each, cloth.

PAUL GERRARD THE CABIN BOY. With Illustrations by PHIZ.

DIGBY HEATHCOTE: the Early Days of a Country Gentleman's Son and Heir. With Illustrations by HARRISON WEIR.

ADVENTURES OF HARRY SKIPWITH BY LAND AND SEA. With Illustrations.

Price 2s. each, cloth.

ADVENTURES IN THE FAR WEST. With Coloured Frontispiece and 36 Illustrations.

ARCTIC ADVENTURES. With Coloured Frontispiece and 40 Illustrations.

ADVENTURES IN AFRICA. By AN AFRICAN TRADER. With Coloured Frontispiece and 42 Illustrations.

ADVENTURES IN INDIA. With Coloured Frontispiece and 36 Illustrations.

KIDNAPPING IN THE PACIFIC. With Coloured Frontispiece and 22 full-page Illustrations.

ADVENTURES IN AUSTRALIA. With Coloured Frontispiece and 34 Illustrations.

THE SWISS FAMILY ROBINSON.
EDITED BY W. H. G. KINGSTON.

The **Five-Shilling Edition.** Printed on fine Paper, with Coloured Plates and 95 Illustrations.

The **Three-and-Sixpenny Edition.** With Coloured Plates and 95 Illustrations.

The **Half-Crown Edition.** With 95 Illustrations.

The **Two-Shilling Edition.** With 95 Illustrations.

LONDON: GEORGE ROUTLEDGE AND SONS,
BROADWAY, LUDGATE HILL.

BOOKS OF TRAVEL AND ADVENTURE.

Price 5s. each, cloth, gilt.

TRAVELLING ABOUT OVER OLD AND NEW GROUND. By LADY BARKER. With Full-page plates.

THE LITTLE SAVAGE. By CAPTAIN MARRYAT. With Illustrations by Sir JOHN GILBERT, R.A.

THE PRAIRIE BIRD. By the Hon. CHARLES MURRAY. With Illustrations by J. B. ZWECKER.

By JULES VERNE.
Price 3s. 6d. each, cloth.

THE ENGLISH AT THE NORTH POLE. With 129 Illustrations by RIOU.

THE FIELD OF ICE. With 126 Illustrations by RIOU.

A VOYAGE ROUND THE WORLD—SOUTH AMERICA. With 71 Illustrations by RIOU.

A VOYAGE ROUND THE WORLD—AUSTRALIA. With 48 Illustrations by RIOU.

A VOYAGE ROUND THE WORLD—NEW ZEALAND, With 46 Illustrations by RIOU.

** Also Cheaper Editions of the above. 1s. each, boards, or 1s. 6d. cloth, gilt edges.

Price 6s. cloth.

THE ADVENTURES OF CAPTAIN HATTERAS. By JULES VERNE. With 250 Illustrations. Being "The English at the North Pole" and "The Field of Ice" in One Volume.

** Also a Cheaper Edition, price 2s. 6d. cloth.

Price 3s. 6d. each, cloth.

A BOY'S ADVENTURES IN THE WILDS OF AUSTRALIA. By WILLIAM HOWITT. With 12 full-page illustrations by HARVEY.

ASCENTS AND ADVENTURES: A Record of Hardy Mountaineering. By HENRY FRITH. With 57 Illustrations.

THE YOUNG MAROONERS. With Illustrations by HARRISON WEIR.

BOY LIFE AMONG THE INDIANS. By the author of "The Young Marooners." With Illustrations.

Price 2s. 6d. cloth.

THE ARCTIC REGIONS. A Narrative of Voyages of Discovery to them. By P. L. SIMMONDS.

THE MARVELS OF THE POLAR WORLD. Translated from the French of E. LESBAZEILLES by ROBERT ROUTLEDGE, B. Sc. (Lond.) F.C.S. With 38 Illustrations.

LONDON: GEORGE ROUTLEDGE AND SONS,
BROADWAY, LUDGATE HILL.

www.ingramcontent.com/pod-product-compliance
Lightning Source LLC
Chambersburg PA
CBHW020844160426
43192CB00007B/773